1986

SYMBOLISM AND INTERPRETATION

Also by Tzvetan Todorov and available in English

The Fantastic: A Structural Approach to a Literary Genre

The Poetics of Prose

Encyclopedic Dictionary of the Sciences of Language
(with Oswald Ducrot)

Theories of the Symbol

TZVETAN TODOROV

SYMBOLISM AND INTERPRETATION

TRANSLATED BY

CATHERINE PORTER

Cornell University Press

ITHACA, NEW YORK

Originally published in French under the title *Symbolisme et interprétation*, ©
1978 Editions du Seuil.

Translation copyright © 1982 by Cornell University Press.

First published 1982 by Cornell University Press.

Printed in the United States of America

*The paper in this book is acid-free and meets the guidelines for permanence and
durability of the Committee on Production Guidelines for Book Longevity of the
Council on Library Resources.*

Library of Congress Cataloging in Publication Data

Todorov, Tzvetan, 1939–
  Symbolism and interpretation.

  Translation of: Symbolisme et interprétation.
  Bibliography: p.
  Includes index.
  1. Hermeneutics. 2. Symbolism. 3. Structural linguistics. I. Title.
BD241.T5813   001.54   82-5078
ISBN 0-8014-1269-2   AACR2

Contents

5

It is just as deadly for the mind to have a system as to have none at all. So one has to make up one's mind to have both.
—Friedrich Schlegel

Verbal Symbolism

Language and Discourse

The distinction between language and discourse is readily apparent to anyone who reflects on the nature of language. Language exists in the abstract; it has a lexicon and grammatical rules as its input and *sentences* as its output. Discourse is a concrete manifestation of language, and it is produced, necessarily, in a specific context that involves not only linguistic elements but also the circumstances of their production: the interlocutors, the time and place, the relations prevailing among these extralinguistic elements. We are no longer concerned with sentences as such, but with sentences that have been produced, or, to put it more succinctly, with *utterances*.

One (short) step further consists in supposing that meaning—in the broadest sense—does not arise in the same way in language and in discourse, in sentences and in utterances, but that it takes sharply distinct forms—so distinct that they should have different names. Thus Beauzée, in the eighteenth century, contrasted *signification* (for language) and *sens* ("meaning"); Emile Benveniste, more recently, spoke of

I should like to acknowledge my indebtedness to two friends: Dan Sperber, whose comments have led me to modify my own thinking in several instances; and Marie-Claude Porcher, who enabled me to become at least somewhat familiar with Sanskrit poetics.

signifiance and *sens.* The signification of a sentence undergoes a double process of determination when the sentence is transformed into an utterance: it loses some of its ambiguity, and its references to the context are made specific. The sentence "John will be here in two hours" certainly has a signification in language, one that is comprehensible to every speaker of English; this signification can be translated into other languages, without any need for supplementary information. But as soon as this sentence becomes an utterance, it begins to refer to a person, to a time, to a place, any or all of which may not be the same the next time the sentence is uttered. Similarly, when used in discourse, words and sentences take on a more specific meaning than they have in language; thus I can speak of "meaning" in Beauzée's sense or in Benveniste's.

A few well-known aphorisms will help bring to mind the long history of the opposition between "signification" (or *signifiance*) and "meaning," and enable us to grasp it better at the same time. Alexander Pope wrote: "I concede that a lexicographer may perhaps know the meaning of a word by itself, but not the meaning of two connected words." And Cicero, very much earlier: "Words have a first value when they are taken in isolation, a second when they are taken together with others. Taken alone, they must be carefully chosen; taken with others, they must be carefully placed." And Montaigne: "I have my own private dictionary."

These three quotations deal with the same distinction, one that is similar at first glance to the one that concerns us here: words are taken either one by one or in groups. The distinction is explicit in the first two texts quoted and implicit in the third: there exists, of course, a dictionary common to all, but the words that make it up take on specific values in the discourse of an individual. Cicero adds an observation concerning the psychic process of production: the selection of lexical entities is the dominant operation at the level of vocabulary;

the combination of lexical entities dominates in sentences. Montaigne's formula is obviously paradoxical: if his dictionary were, as he claims, entirely personal and private, cut off from that of other users of the language, how could he communicate this very information? But it is clear that the thought is paradoxical only in its expression, for want of two different terms to designate meaning, one for language and the other for discourse. Yet above and beyond these nuances separating our three authors, their unity stands out just as clearly: the opposition each one has in mind is related to the distinction between language and discourse, but does not correspond to it precisely, and this noncoincidence provides a good way to characterize a certain classical conception of language. For the classical author, the important boundary lies between words and sentences, not between language and discourse; or, to put it another way, language is reduced to words (just as, for Saussure, there are no sentences in "language" [langue]). Whereas for us, instead, words and sentences together are opposed to utterances.

Direct and Indirect Meaning

The foregoing is all somewhat self-evident, but I needed to mention it here before approaching my specific concern: namely, that each utterance can be used and interpreted in a quite different way. Rather than meaning "John will be here in two hours" (whatever John, here, and now I may have in mind), I may produce the same utterance in order to transmit some very different information; for example: "We have to get out of here before then." Such an interpretation is possible only for a particular utterance and in a concrete context; thus we remain in the realm of discourse and of utterances. But whereas the "meaning" proper to discourse and discussed above would deserve to be called "direct," this latter is an *indirect* discursive meaning grafted onto the former. I reserve the name *verbal symbolism* for the area of indirect meaning, and the name *symbolics of language* for the study of these meanings. The negative prefix in "indirect" should not be allowed to suggest a marginal phenomenon, an occasional appendage of direct meaning. Indirect production of meaning is present in all discourse, and in some kinds of discourse, including some important ones, it is probably wholly dominant—for example, in everyday conversation, or in literature.

To discover in the past a wide-ranging and incisive discussion of the problems of indirect language use, we have to step outside the Western frame of reference and turn to the Indian tradition (whose spirit informs the pages that follow). At some point during the twelfth century, the Sanskrit poetician Mammata (Kāvyaprakāśa) summarized as follows the prevailing ideas of his day—ideas engendered by the fundamental work of Ānandavardhana, who was perhaps the greatest of all theorists of textual symbolism. Mammata identified seven differences between direct expression and indirect suggestion:

(1) Difference in the nature of the statement: the expressed meaning prohibits or denies, for example, while the suggested meaning commands or affirms.

(2) Difference in time: the suggested meaning is grasped after the expressed meaning.

(3) Difference in the linguistic material: the expressed meaning emanates from words; the suggested meaning may arise from a sound, a sentence, or an entire work.

(4) Difference in the means of apprehension: the expressed meaning is understood by means of grammatical rules, whereas the suggested meaning requires a context as well: spatio-temporal circumstances, an interlocutor, and so on.

(5) Difference in effect: the expressed meaning brings about a simple cognitive perception; the suggested meaning also produces charm.

(6) Difference in number: the expressed meaning is univocal; the suggested meaning may be plurivalent.

(7) Difference in the person addressed: the expressed meaning may well be addressed to one character, the suggested meaning to another.

To our eyes, these differences do not all appear to be on the same level. One of them (difference 4) concerns not the opposition between direct and indirect evocation, but the one between language and discourse: every discourse, whether or not it is suggestive, implies a reference to the context of enunciation. Others are simply clarifications of the basic difference between expression and suggestion: the interlocutor may not be the same (7), or the statement may be different (1). Still another concerns the effect produced by the utterance, rather than its structure (5). But the three remaining oppositions give a good description of the properties of the symbolic process: difference in *linguistic dimensions*; difference in *number of meanings*; finally, difference in the *order of appearance*—the indirect is grafted, by definition, onto the direct, it presupposes anteriority, thus temporality. Conversely, to affirm the posteriority of the symbolic is to define it as being what is indirect. The pages that follow will be devoted to the examination of these various aspects and phases of the symbolic process.

Two Denials of the Symbolic

But before we embark upon detailed description, several general questions ought to be raised. We need, first of all, to inquire whether those who reject the very existence of an opposition between direct and indirect meaning may not be right after all.

The opposition has indeed been challenged, sometimes implicitly, from two very different viewpoints. The first is, on the whole, the viewpoint of linguists (with some exceptions, needless to say, and some tendency toward change in recent years); it is denial by nonrecognition. Works on linguistic or semantic theory do no more, at best, than signal their own lack of attention to marginal cases of linguistic usage such as metaphor, irony, or allusion. This position would be defensible if it were based on a distinction between language and discourse, and thus on an appeal for discourse analysis at least; but such is not the case. The exclusions are justified on the basis of empiricist principles that are first simplified to the point of caricature, then assimilated without reservation: only what is perceptible, only what is directly accessible to the senses exists (or, in any case, nothing else counts)—thus there is no question of indirect meaning.

The other critique reverses the situation. Where a moment ago we found only direct meaning, now we find only indirect. Beginning probably with the romantic rejection of hierarchies, a Nietzsche or his current descendants say that there is no such thing as proper meaning, that all is metaphor; there are differences in degree only, not in kind. Words never grasp the essence of things, but only evoke them indirectly. However, if everything is metaphor, then nothing is. And these two critiques, starting from such incompatible viewpoints, converge, curiously enough, in their conclusion, in which they deny the specificity of verbal symbolism and thus deny its existence. The geometry of meaning is reduced, in both cases, to a single dimension.

If I reject these two opposing viewpoints in turn, if I persist in believing in the existence of symbolic phenomena, it is not because I consider myself the possessor of a philosophical truth superior to the empiricism of the one camp or to the dogmatism of the other; it is rather because my intuition as a subject engaged in verbal exchange does not allow me to assimilate two instances so different as when I say "It is cold in here" to signify that it is cold in here, and when I produce the same sentence in order to suggest that someone ought to close the window. Or again, when the sentence "You are my proud and generous lion" is addressed by a lioness (with the gift of speech) to her husband, and when the same sentence comes from a woman's mouth and is addressed to Hernani, in Victor Hugo's play. I take the capacity to observe this difference to be a characteristic feature of the human mind; and I take the attempt to understand it to be the objective of any theory of verbal symbolism.

Verbal and Nonverbal

I always add the adjective "verbal" to the substantive "symbolism" because, like so many other people, I believe that a nonverbal symbolism exists. To be more precise: the symbolic phenomenon is in no way specifically linguistic; it is merely conveyed by language. Secondary or indirect meanings are evoked by association; this was well known in antiquity, when tropes and associations were classified in the same manner. Now association is a psychic process that is certainly not specifically linguistic: we associate objects, or actions, as well as words, and a situation may be symbolic; so may a gesture. There exists no "metaphorical meaning" in language irreducible to linguistic meaning in general and to translinguistic processes such as association. Meanings evoked indirectly are meanings like any others; they differ only in their mode of evocation, which is precisely that of the association of something present with something absent. Schleiermacher had already seen this clearly: "Words used in the figurative sense retain their proper and specific meaning, and achieve their effect only through an association of ideas on which the writer depends."

One might nevertheless advance the following argument: it would suffice to concede the nonspecificity of meaning—to admit, therefore, that meaning is no more than an association between signifier and signified—in order to justify a countermove in which we would transfer all we know about meaning back to the realm of symbolism; and, although recognizing the existence of a nonverbal symbolism, we would see all symbolism cast in the likeness of language. This is, I think, the perhaps implicit reasoning that underlies the recent expansion of "semiotics." But such an assimilation entails a double loss. For meaning is not simply an association like any other. Association implies the possibility of conceiving of each of the associated entities autonomously. Now the signifier exists only because it has a signified, and vice versa; they are not two freely existing entities that someone has decided to link together at a given moment. Thus, by treating meaning as an association, we make precise knowledge of it impossible. At the same time, the specificity of symbolic processes is obscured when the categorization (or, more benignly, the terminology) appropriate to language and meaning is imposed upon them; for even if those who hold this view make an initial concession, adding symbolic water to the wine of meaning, they nonetheless go on to project the specific features of language onto a quite distinct realm, that of symbolism. To speak at every turn of "language" and of "meaning" is thus possible only if we empty these terms of their specific (and only interesting) content.

Sign, Symbol

This brings us back to the problematic *sign/symbol* pair. We might begin by looking at the descriptions offered in the past, to see how well founded they are.

The most widespread theory, extending from Plato to Saussure, locates the difference exclusively in motivation, which would be present in the one case and absent in the other; the signifier either resembles or does not resemble the signified. But one cannot speak of motivation (that is, of a type of association) in the case of linguistic meaning; to do so would be to compare incomparable entities. Furthermore, motivation may be more or less present, more or less lost to memory; that does not prevent a symbol from remaining a symbol.

Another theory, of equally ancient origin but one that has become popular especially since the romantics (for them, the duality is often that of "symbol" and "allegory," the latter taking the place of "sign"), locates the difference in the *inexhaustible* character of the symbol, the clear and univocal character of the sign (or of allegory). In this case, one of the consequences of the process is turned into a description of the process itself: association may indeed be indefinitely extended, unlike the signifier-signified relationship which is by nature closed; but in order to understand this fact, we first have to see that there is association, grafted (or not) onto signification.

Thus the idea of the direct sign and the indirect symbol—in itself a very old idea, held by Clement of Alexandria and Saint Augustine—gives us a better understanding of the facts. But we might wonder whether it is of any use at all even to couple these two terms, given that in so doing we imply a preexisting entity that would then split apart into sign and symbol. The two notions are not situated on the same level, and in fact they cannot be compared. Semiotics has no reason to exist, I am afraid, if it is to be the common framework of semantics (of language) and of symbolics: we do not form *one* new thing in combining, for example, the sun and plants; "semiotics," then, appears acceptable to me only to the extent that it is synonymous with "symbolics."

Verbal, Symbolic

Let us backtrack. Why persist in studying *verbal* symbolism, rather than symbolism, period, and thus persist in giving undue importance to what is only one mode of transmission among others? The answer, for me, is twofold.

First, the knowledge we already have of verbal symbolism is incomparably richer than our knowledge of other forms of symbolism. (This knowledge is dispersed, to be sure, among fields as diverse as logic and poetics, rhetoric and hermeneutics.) Then, linguistic symbolism is the easiest to handle (words on a page as opposed, let us say, to animals in a circus or the customs of a society) while at the same time it is probably the most complex manifestation of symbolism. These reasons are strategically important, but they must not be allowed to obscure the contingent nature of the connection between the terms "verbal" and "symbolism."

Association, although we did not find it in linguistic meaning, is not absent from linguistics (even apart from the symbolic phenomena). It must be sought not in the relations between signifier and signified but in the relations between words or between sentences: relations of coordination and subordination, predication and determination, generalization and entailment. The idea of a common framework for the study of verbal phenomena of this sort and of symbolic phenomena such as tropes or allusion, even if it is not often explicitly affirmed, is nonetheless present in the classical tradition. Aristotle classifies tropes exactly as he does syllogisms. The classical theory of "accessory ideas" (from the Port-Royal *Logic* through Du Marsais to Condillac) makes it possible to deal on the same level with the relation between subject and predicate on the one hand, the relation between proper meaning and figurative meaning on the other. Differences exist, of course, and the discovery of a common framework also enables us to locate these differences with greater precision: they all stem from the fact that the associated terms are *both* present in discourse, whereas *only one* of them is present in symbolic evocation. As a result (I say this without too much hope that my usage will be universally adopted), the receiver *understands* discourses but *interprets* symbols.

Symbolism and Interpretation

I should like indeed to postulate the *inseparability of symbolism and interpretation* (Paul Ricoeur does this too). These are, for me, simply two aspects (production and reception) of a single phenomenon. Consequently, I do not believe that it is desirable or even possible to study them in isolation. A text or a discourse becomes symbolic at the point when, through an effort of interpretation, we discover in it an indirect meaning. Schelling wrote: "The charm of Homeric poetry and of all mythology rests, to tell the truth, on the fact that they also contain allegorical signification as a *possibility*—one could also allegorize everything." One could, and that possibility is essential. But we do not do so, for all that; in principle, we require that the text itself indicate to us its symbolic nature, that it possess a series of observable and undeniable properties through which it leads us on to that peculiar form of reading which is "interpretation." We begin with the answer, with the interpretive reaction, but we go back to the question, which is posed by the symbolic nature of the text itself.

The production and the reception of discourse have given rise, in the past, to two separate disciplines, rhetoric and hermeneutics. Fortunately, these two bodies of knowledge have not always been maintained in a deplorable isolation. The verb *herméneuein* originally designated the activity of producing discourse quite as much as it referred to the understanding of discourse—if not more so. Augustine started with the categories of Ciceronian rhetoric when he set in place the first great Christian hermeneutics. And through a precisely symmetrical gesture Du Marsais inaugurated the last brilliant period of rhetoric thirteen centuries later, transferring the hermeneutic categories elaborated in the meantime back into the framework of rhetoric (as if the passage from the profane to the sacred were necessarily accompanied by the passage from production to reception). Schleiermacher, the founder of general hermeneutics, explicitly affirmed the unity of these two disciplines: "The kinship of rhetoric and hermeneutics consists in the fact that every act of comprehension is the inverse of an act of speech." (His contemporary, Ast, for his part, wrote: "Understanding and explaining a work is a veritable reproduction or reconstruction of what has already been constructed.") The *types* of discourse, or the choices among all the possibilities offered to textual production, have their counterpart in the interpretive *strategies*, or ways of reading, that have been codified by the various exegetic schools. F. A. Wolf remarked that "the explication of a poet has different rules from those appropriate to a prose-writer"; Friedrich Schlegel wondered whether we might also have "an epic, a lyric, a dramatic philology"; and on the basis of the various attitudes that have been taken toward texts, Schleiermacher himself established a veritable typology of discourse, extending from the lyric through the epistolary, the didactic, and the historical to the scientific.

Two Levels of Generality

My presentation is divided into two parts, "Symbolics of Language" and "Strategies of Interpretation." This division is not the product of a distinction between the two viewpoints, symbolism and interpretation; on the contrary, these viewpoints will be found in concert throughout the book. The division is rather a function of a distinction between two *levels:* that of the *general theory,* which attempts to account for all possible phenomena within its purview, and that of the *particular strategy,* whether of production or of reception (even though I myself am especially concerned with the latter), a "strategy" which consists precisely in choosing, on the basis of specified criteria, among all the possibilities that are offered to us at each moment. The question of strategies will be examined at length in Part II; it should suffice for now to indicate, by means of two examples to which I shall not return, what the difference in level consists of, and why certain distinctions have to be integrated at the level of strategy rather than at the level of the general theory.

Leo Strauss writes, at the beginning of one of his essays (in *Persecution and the Art of Writing*):

> To understand the words of another man, living or dead, may mean two different things which for the moment we shall call interpretation and explanation. By interpretation we mean the attempt to ascertain what the speaker said and how he actually understood what he said, regardless of whether he expressed that understanding explicitly or not. By explanation we mean the attempt to ascertain those implications of his statements of which he was unaware. Accordingly, the realization that a given statement is ironical, or a lie, belongs to the interpretation of the statement, whereas the realization that a given statement is based on a mistake, or is the unconscious expression of a wish, an interest, a bias, or a historical situation, belongs to its explanation.[1]

The important distinction, for Strauss, is not between direct and indirect meaning, since both of these are on the side of what he calls "interpretation," but between two forms of indirect meaning: the one intended by the author, and the one that remains unconscious for the author (this latter closely resembles what Louis Althusser more recently has called "symptomal reading"). Another theorist of interpretation, E. D. Hirsch, writes: "*Meaning* is that which is presented by a text; it is what the author meant by his use of a particular sign sequence. *Significance*, on the other hand, names a relationship between that meaning and a person, or a conception, or a situation, or indeed anything imaginable."[2] The "meaning" is the internal meaning of the work, which includes indirect as well as direct meaning (the author uses

---

[1] *Persecution and the Art of Writing* (Westport, Conn., 1973), p. 143.
[2] *Validity in Interpretation* (New Haven, 1967), p. 8.

metaphor, irony, and innuendo quite intentionally), whereas "significance" results from the inclusion of the work in another context. Here again, the distinction crosses through what I call indirect meaning, separating two forms of it, the one centripetal and the other centrifugal. Such distinctions may be more or less well founded, may lead to more or less interesting results. What matters to me in the present context is that they are situated from the outset on a level different from the one on which I have chosen to operate. Whether they take the viewpoint of production (Hirsch) or of reception (Strauss), they introduce external norms into the field of the morphology of symbolic or interpretive forms. These norms allow us to distinguish, through a kind of projection, between types of meaning or understanding; and they lead, finally, in a way that is not always explicit but that is no less important on that account, toward value judgments. We are well aware that "explanation" has a different value from that of "interpretation" in Leo Strauss's eyes, just as "meaning" is more worthy of respect than is "significance" for E. D. Hirsch.

My Ambition

My ambition, in the pages that follow, is to show why diverse interpretations are possible and how they function, rather than to valorize certain of these interpretations or even to group them in relation to a given norm. Rather than being normative, I have tried to remain descriptive, insofar as possible. I have no new "theory of the symbol" or "theory of interpretation" to propose (perhaps because I have spent too much time reading those of others). I have tried to establish a framework that makes it possible to understand how so many different theories, so many irreconcilable subdivisions, so many contradictory definitions, can have existed—each one including (this is my hypothesis) a measure of truth, but a truth which has emerged only at the price of bracketing off other aspects of the same phenomenon. I have not attempted to decide what a symbol is, nor an allegory, nor how to find the "correct" interpretation; but I have tried to understand, and if possible to maintain, the complex and the plural.

Part I

SYMBOLICS OF LANGUAGE

The kinship of rhetoric and hermeneutics consists
in the fact that every act of comprehension is
the inverse of an act of speech.
—Friedrich Schleiermacher

The Decision to Interpret

Accommodation, Assimilation

Every psychic process, we are told, includes two phases or aspects, which Piaget labels *accommodation* and *assimilation*. The human psyche is endowed with certain characteristic schemas that are always available, and when it is confronted with unfamiliar actions and situations it reacts, on the one hand, by adapting old schemas to the new object (accommodation) and, on the other, by adapting the new phenomenon to old schemas (assimilation).

The interpretive process likewise includes these two phases (which occur here in a fixed order). First, we have to distinguish the verbal sequence for which interpretation is required; this perception of difference is itself conditioned by the fact that the sequence cannot be absorbed by the available schemas; thus in an initial phase we recognize the new phenomenon while adapting to it (accommodation). Then we absorb this novelty and this nonintegrability, until the verbal sequence comes into conformity with already-constructed schemas (assimilation). This is something that the Sanskrit poeticians understand well. Mammaṭa summarizes their position as follows: it is necessary, first, that an incompatibility between the primary meaning of the word and its context be manifest; second, that a relation of association exist between the primary and secondary meanings.

27

In my discussion I shall follow this bipartite division, devoting this chapter to the first phase—to the conditions necessary for the making of a decision to interpret—and in the following chapters examining the essential aspects of the symbolic association itself.

The Principle of Pertinence

In order to account for the triggering of the interpretive process, we must assume at the outset that the production and reception of discourse (of utterances, and not of sentences) obey a very general rule of pertinence, according to which if a discourse exists there must be a reason for it. So that when at first glance a given discourse does not obey this rule, the receiver's spontaneous reaction is to determine whether the discourse might not reveal its pertinence through some particular manipulation. "Interpretation" (still in the narrow sense) is what we call this manipulation.

Philosophers of language have recently drawn attention to the existence of such a principle, although they have usually limited themselves to particular cases of verbal exchange rather than encompassing the totality of discursive production. H. P. Grice, analyzing the "logic of conversation," has suggested that conversation obeys a rule of cooperation that may be formulated as follows: "Make your conversation contribution such as is required, at the stage at which it occurs, by the accepted purpose or direction of the talk-exchange in which you are engaged" (p. 45).[1] If A asks B how C's work is going, and B replies: "Fine; he's not in jail yet," the response is non-pertinent. But since there is no reason for B to violate the rule of cooperation, A will look for some way to make the response pertinent, and will find a complement: "even though C is dishonest." We recognize the technique of allu-

[1]For this and for other passages quoted, page references will be included in my text when the work in question appears in the bibliography, pp. 171–172.

sion here; what leads us to look for allusion is indeed a certain incoherence in the conversational sequence.

Oswald Ducrot describes the same process, examining in this case not the relation between two successive remarks, but the isolated utterance.

> The central theme of these laws, in our linguistic community, is that speech is motivated, that people do not speak just for the sake of speaking (which is considered a failing) nor in order to carry out a ritual (which is considered a superstition), but because there is some use in doing it, either for the speaker or the listener or some third party. . . . From this arises the possibility, which is always open, of incorporating and of seeking "allusions" in any discourse at all. To praise Peter to Paul can always "look like" setting Peter up as a model for Paul. To mention the time to someone may (since we do not speak "for no reason") amount to asking him to leave. [*Dire et ne pas dire*, pp. 10, 11]

The principle of pertinence of which I am speaking is nothing more than a generalization of what Grice calls cooperation and Ducrot calls motivation.

It is not always easy to define the nature of pertinence, however. Grice and Ducrot refer to "natural" reactions: universal and eternal ones. That remains true, no doubt, for the principle itself; but the content of the norms of pertinence is variable (it is a function of the observer's ideological framework). If it is relatively easy to agree on what is not pertinent (and consequently calls for interpretation), it is on the other hand almost impossible to establish with certainty that a given utterance *is* sufficiently pertinent, and that it therefore does not authorize interpretation. The field of the interpretable is always threatening to grow larger. These extensions are justified, on the side of interpretation, by reference to an *ideological framework,* and, on the side of production, by submission to a *genre*—which, as August Boeckh had already seen, is nothing more than a contract established between author and reader, one that in fact determines the type

29

of reading to be adopted (a supernatural event has to be interpreted in a realistic narrative, but does not need interpretation in a fantasy). I shall leave aside here the question of genres, which has been very thoroughly studied in recent times.

In Search of Textual Indices

Reference to the ideological framework, which makes it possible to determine the threshold of pertinence, is not always presented as such; it prefers to hide behind objective properties of the text: in this way we return to production. We can thus observe that, throughout the history of exegesis, people have attempted to base the decision to interpret on the presence of a certain number of specifically textual indices (not to mention cases in which the originator of the utterance indicates metalinguistically that interpretation is required, by giving his text a title such as "Allegory," or by opening his discourse as Christ does: Now I shall speak in parables). We might divide these indices (the word must be taken in the sense it has in hermeneutics: it designates the means of marking textual status, and thereby of inducing a certain form of reading) into two large groups: they derive from the establishment of a relation between the given segment and either other utterances belonging to the same *context* (syntagmatic indices) or else the shared knowledge of a community, with its *collective memory* (paradigmatic indices). Appearances notwithstanding, this latter does not lead us beyond the text.

Syntagmatic Indices

When the indices are to be sought in the relations between the utterance and its syntagmatic context, we can identify two further groupings, which I shall call indices based on lack and indices based on excess. *Based on lack:* the clearest example is that of contradiction; every time two segments of a text contradict each other, the interpreter will be tempted to transform the meaning of one or the other (or both). It is also necessary to reckon with that weakened form of contradiction which is discontinuity (within a sentence, between sentences, between paragraphs, and so on), whether it is actually semantic or rather stylistic. *Based on excess:* the extreme case is that of tautology, and it is well known that tautologies in common usage (a dollar's a dollar, and the like) imply different interpretations for each occurrence of the same word. The same is true for repetition, or for its most widespread variant, superfluity: but here we return to the principle of pertinence itself, stripped of linguistic justifications.

Paradigmatic Indices

As for the indices arising from a confrontation between a given utterance and the collective memory of a society, we can likewise distinguish several types, according to the nature of the shared knowledge referred to. There is, first of all, the case of whatever is unintelligible, incomprehensible with the help of the common dictionary and grammar, and with respect to which one of two attitudes must be adopted: it may be ignored, or interpreted. Then comes all the common knowledge establishing the limits of what is (scientifically) possible, at a given historical moment; this is what is (materially) plausible in a society, and every time a given utterance runs counter to it, we may attempt to interpret the utterance in order to bring it back into harmony with the plausible. Finally, there is the culturally plausible, that is, the set of norms and values that determine what is appropriate within a society; improprieties may be absorbed by interpretation (the reference to the ideological framework is scarcely disguised here).

There is one other way to refer to the culturally plausible, but in this case we can dispense with indices, as it were: a large number of inferences have become automatic, the pres-

31

ence of the antecedent invariably provoking that of the consequent, or vice versa. The following sentences appear in the first chapter of Tolstoy's *Hadji Murat:*

> Hadji Murat was a lieutenant of Shamil renowned for his exploits against the Russians. He always rode into battle under his own banner, accompanied by dozens of murids prancing around him. Now, clad in a hooded cap and cloak, with a gun-band jutting out, he rode with a single murid, trying to attract as little notice as possible and glancing warily with his quick dark eyes at the faces of the villagers whom he met on the road.[2]

Hadji Murat's furtive behavior is automatically associated for us with the presence of danger and with the desire to hide: the one evokes the other without a need for any index whatsoever that would invite interpretation. In "psychological" novels, the reader infers and constructs the characters' personalities in just the same way.

Examples of Symbolism

I shall take several examples of textual or exegetic practices in order to illustrate the foregoing distinctions.

In the mystic poetry of Saint John of the Cross, the problem is posed as follows. At first glance, the text is speaking of physical love and makes no mention of spiritual notions; on the other hand, we know from the commentaries that the author himself supplies with the texts and from the overall context of their production that the texts in question are indeed mystical, and deal with divine love. But does the text itself supply indices that invite interpretation? We read in the *Spiritual Canticle* (the title is obviously a first crucial index):[3]

[2]Lev N. Tolstoy, *Hadji Murat*, trans. W. G. Carey (London, 1962), p. 10.
[3]Trans. E. Allison Peers (Garden City, N.Y., 1961). The passages quoted are from stanzas 3, 5, 2, and 1 respectively.

> [I was] without light or guide,
> save that which burned in my heart

and a few lines further on:

> Oh, night that guided me!

The one and only guide is at one point called "night," at another "light . . . which . . . burned in my heart." If we grant that there is but one guide and if we assume that the discourse conforms to the principle of pertinence, we shall be led to the following conclusion: night, or light, or both, must not be taken in their literal meanings (apart from the fact that they are not only different but opposed to each other).

Other indices are less clear. Two lines of the second stanza describe a single event:

> [I went out]
> In darkness and secure
> . . .
> In darkness and in concealment

If assurance seems oddly paired with dissimulation, this is only a matter of cultural plausibility. Nothing in this passage is impossible; and yet one is tempted to seek a second meaning in this "exit." Likewise, when the subject describes himself

> Kindled in love with yearnings
> —oh, happy chance!—

the combination of yearnings and happiness jars only our prevailing psychological notions; but that counts.

A page from Maeterlinck's *Pelleas and Melisande* will familiarize us with other indices that point to a secondary meaning:

Golaud: Who has hurt you?
Melisande: Every one! every one!
Golaud: What hurt have they done you?
Melisande: I cannot tell! I cannot tell!
Golaud: Come; do not weep so. Whence come you?
Melisande: I have fled!... fled!... fled!...
Golaud: Yes; but whence have you fled?
Melisande: I am lost!... lost!... Oh! oh! lost here... I am not
of this place... I was not born there....
Golaud: Whence are you? Where were you born?
Melisande: Oh! oh! far away from here!... far away... far
away....[4]

This time the indices are very obvious; perhaps it is not by
chance that we are dealing with a *symbolist* drama. The first
index is repetition: Melisande repeats almost everything she
says. Would she do this if her words had only their ordinary
meaning? Is this not an invitation to seek a second, "deeper"
meaning? Then there is discontinuity: Melisande scarcely answers any of the questions asked. Later on in the same scene
we witness exchanges of the following sort: Golaud: "Why do
you look so astonished?" Melisande: "Are you a giant?" Or,
again: Golaud: "How old are you?" Melisande: "I am beginning to be cold...." One other peculiarity of Melisande's
remarks plays an important role: their indeterminacy, which
calls the imagination of the reader or listener into play. Her
statements are either overtly negative ("I cannot tell," "I am
not of this place") or extremely vague in their reference ("far
from here..."). To these characteristics, of course, certain
elements of the graphic code are added: exclamation points
and suspension points.

An entirely different type of index confronts us in the
worldly salons of the late nineteenth century, such as Henry
James describes in *The Awkward Age.* Here is an exchange
between Mrs. Brookenham and her daughter Nanda:

[4]Trans. Richard Hovey (New York, 1915), p. 23.

"Why, she [the Duchess] has never had to pay for *any*thing."
"And do you mean that *you* have had to pay?" . . .⁵

Mrs. Brook's sentence is neither contradictory nor repetitive, and it does not evoke any implausible event. Her daughter nevertheless considers herself justified in interpreting it as if it contained an implication: for, otherwise, this sentence would have broken the rule that disallows any superfluity. The threshold of pertinence is raised very high in Mrs. Brook's salon: one does not say "X is such-and-such" except to suggest: "but *I* am not"; otherwise, the utterance would have been flat, and useless.

Let us reread these two consecutive sentences in the prologue to Tolstoy's *Hadji Murat:*

> "What energy," I thought; "man has conquered everything, destroying millions of blades of grass, yet this fellow is still undefeated." Then I remembered an old story from the Caucasus, part of which I have seen, part heard from eye-witnesses, and part completed in my imagination. [P. 9]

The narrator sees a thistle in the field, then he remembers a story. No explicit relation links these two events. And yet their very succession in the narrator's mind, or (what is in effect the same thing) in the text being read, is enough to indicate that there is indeed a relationship between the two. And indeed, since this relationship is not causal and narrative, it can only be textual and symbolic: we are invited to interpret the thistle as the allegorical image of the being whose story we are about to hear. This is achieved simply by reference to the principle of pertinence, according to which no sentence, no sequence of sentences can be gratuitous: it is not that "birds of a feather flock together" (cf. the French proverb *qui se ressemble s'assemble*), but that "birds that flock

⁵*The Novels and Tales of Henry James* (New York, 1980), 9: 318–319.

together are of a feather," that is, resemble each other (*qui s'assemble se ressemble*).

Examples of Interpretation

Let us now see how one proceeds in an exegetical school. First of all, a philosophical doctrine may come up with the postulate that everything is to be interpreted; in this case, textual indices can be dispensed with, and the process becomes so simple that one can hardly even speak of exegetical rules. This is the situation with medieval symbolism, in which the whole universe is assumed to be symbolic of God (the world is a book): no particular index is needed to set interpretation in motion. The situation of Platonism is somewhat similar: in this case, visible phenomena are necessarily incarnations of immaterial ideas. Making all due allowances, we can say the same thing of psychoanalytic interpretation.

Religious or sacred exegesis, although endowed with an exorbitant appetite, has sought to formulate relatively limited criteria. The type of index most frequently cited is inappropriateness: a text must be interpreted because otherwise it would not illustrate divine holiness. The spurious Heraclitus could already say of Homer, whose epic had come to play the role of a sacred text: "All is impiety in Homer if he has not used allegory"—a scandalous situation to which, indeed, the allegorical remedy will be applied. And J. G. Frazer is right to argue that the history of religions is nothing but a long effort to reconcile an ancient practice with a new justification, and that, in our field, this effort takes the form of interpretation.

Reading Philo of Alexandria, we may observe the nature of the indices on which a typical example of religious exegesis is based (my quotations are from the *Legum allegoria*):[6]

[6] "Allegorical Interpretation of Genesis II., III.," in *Philo*, trans. F. H. Colson and G. H. Whitaker (London, 1929), vol. 1.

Contradiction:

Nevertheless Adam is not naked now: "they made for themselves girdles" are the words that occur a little further back. Even by this it is the prophet's wish to teach thee, that he understands by nakedness not that of the body, but that by which the mind is found unprovided and unclothed with virtue. [III, 55]

Discontinuity:

"And God said to the woman, 'What is this thou hast done?' And she said, 'The serpent beguiled me and I ate' " (Gen. iii. 13). God puts a question to sense-perception touching one point, she gives an answer touching another point: for God asks something about the man; she speaks not about him, but says something about herself, for her words are "I ate," not "I gave." Perhaps, then as we read the passage figuratively, we shall solve the puzzle and show that the woman gives a very pertinent answer to the question put to her. [III, 59–60]

Superfluity:

Why, after saying before "green of the field," does he go on to say "and all grass," as if it were impossible for green of the field to come up as grass? The fact is, "the green of the field" is the 'intellectually-perceptible,' an outgrowth of the mind, but the "grass" is the 'sensibly-perceptible,' it in turn being a growth of the unreasoning part of the soul. [I, 24]

Implausibility:

One of these women is the wife of Potiphar, Pharaoh's head-cook (Gen. xxxix. 1 ff.). How, being a eunuch, he comes to have a wife, is a point to be considered: for those, who are occupied with the literal wording of the law rather than with its figurative interpretation, will find that it involves what appears to [be] such a difficulty. [III, 236]

Inappropriateness:

> God forbid that we should be infected with such monstrous
> folly as to think that God employs for inbreathing organs such
> as mouth or nostrils; for God is not only not in the form of man,
> but belongs to no class or kind. Yet the expression clearly brings
> out something that accords with nature. [I, 36–37]

And so on...

Modern literary criticism bases its interpretive practice on postulates advanced by the romantic aesthetic, first and foremost on that of organic form (to such an extent that it might well be labeled "organic criticism"). Everything in a work corresponds to everything else, everything tends toward a single "figure in the carpet," and the best interpretation is the one that allows for the integration of the greatest number of textual elements. Thus we are ill equipped to read discontinuity, incoherence, the unintegrable.

Finally, one can imagine a case in which no specific indices are present, nor any global principle requiring interpretation—and yet the subject does not cease to interpret.... The case exists, but it falls outside the accepted exegetical strategies: it is what psychopathologists call the "interpretive delirium," and it is a form of paranoia. Which suggests, conversely, that our society does indeed require motivation for every decision to interpret.

The Role of Linguistic Structure

Once the decision to interpret has been made, the interpreter plunges into symbolic association (or "evocation"),
which allows him to assimilate the strangeness that he has
noted: such an evocation has numerous facets. Rather than
attempting to rationalize this multiplicity, in each of the chapters that follow I shall examine one of the five major categories
that it seems to me indispensable to single out, in order to pur-
sue the simultaneously general and particular discussion that I
have begun here. The first group of problems that I shall
study has to do with the effect of the linguistic structure of the
interpretable segment on the very process of interpretation.
And to begin with: if we limit ourselves to distinctions within
the verbal material, do forms of verbal symbolism result?

Lexical Symbolism and Propositional Symbolism

In the rabbinical commentaries on the Pentateuch, we find
the following example: It is stated in the Bible that even animals will be rewarded by God; and the commentary adds:
"And can one not reason *a fortiori* that if it is so for a beast,
how much more rightly then for man will God not withhold
his reward?" A single proposition is presented in the text
under discussion: "animals will be rewarded"; but this proposition allows us (a) to understand its meaning, which is that

animals will be rewarded, and (b) to give it a secondary, indirect interpretation, which is that *men* will be rewarded. Let us set aside the device of a fortiori, or qal wahômèr, which is essential in the rabbinical gloss, and retain the overall result: the signifier of a single proposition leads us to knowledge of two signifieds, one direct and the other indirect.

Now let us suppose that in the proposition "animals will be rewarded" the term "animals" is used metaphorically to designate, for example, the meek. The word "animal" will evoke on the one hand, directly, the meaning *animal*; on the other hand, indirectly, that of *meek*. A single signifier will lead us once again to knowledge of two signifieds.

Linguistic symbolism is defined by this overflowing of the signifier by the signified; thus we now have two examples of the symbolic functioning of language. What they have in common is obvious. How do they differ? The difference lies in the nature of the linguistic unit that is to be subjected to the symbolic process: this unit may or may not allow the directly formulated statement to be maintained. In the first case, where the statement is maintained, the initial proposition "the animals will be rewarded" can be put to the test of truthfulness; in the second case, on the other hand, it does not make sense to wonder whether animals in the literal sense will really be rewarded or not. The question does not arise; only the proposition concerning men can be considered true or false. Or again, if we wanted to make explicit everything that these two segments convey, we would have, in the first case: (1) animals will be rewarded; (2) men are like animals (only better); (3) men will be rewarded too: three propositions. And, in the second: (1) some men are like animals; (2) these men will be rewarded: two propositions. In the first case, the element being interpreted is a *proposition*, whereas in the second case we have a lesser element: a *word* or a phrase. I shall speak of *propositional symbolism* to designate cases like the first one, and of *lexical symbolism* for cases like the second; we must keep in mind that "lexical" does not refer here to the lexicon (which belongs to language, not to discourse, and from which, consequently, all symbolic effect is absent), but to words or phrases, segments that are shorter than propositions and that do not make any statement in and of themselves.

History of the Opposition

To my knowledge, no one in the Western tradition has attempted to juxtapose and to distinguish these two linguistic phenomena in (precisely) this way. Which does not mean that the distinction itself has gone unnoticed; but it has been described in other ways, less satisfying ones, as I shall attempt to show.

The best-known description has its origin in the writings of the fathers of the church. Clement of Alexandria seems to have been the first to formulate our distinction, not between two forms of symbolism, but between two possible definitions of the phenomenon of symbolism:

> Wherefore also He employed metaphorical description; for such is the parable,—a narration based on some subject which is not the principal subject, but similar to the principal subject, and leading him who understands to what is the true and principal thing; or, as some say, a mode of speech presenting with vigor, by means of other circumstances, what is the principal subject. [*The Miscellanies*, VI, XV][1]

The parable can be described *either* as the evocation of one object which in turn evokes another; *or* as an expression endowed with several meanings, some of which are direct and others indirect.

[1] *The Miscellanies*, in *The Writings of Clement of Alexandria*, trans. William Wilson, The Ante-Nicene Christian Library, vol. XII, (Edinburgh, 1869), 2: 378–379.

The same possibility of providing a double description of a single phenomenon appears in the writings of Augustine, that great synthesizer of earlier traditions. In *On Christian Doctrine*, among other things, he integrates the rhetorical heritage to a general semiological theory; tropes acquire the status of "transposed signs" (*signa translata*).[2] But Augustine no longer defines trope the way the rhetoricians did (as a word used in a sense that does not normally belong to it). He writes:

> Figurative signs occur when that thing which we designate by a literal sign is used to signify something else; thus we say "ox" and by that syllable understand the animal which is ordinarily designated by that word, but again by that animal we understand an evangelist, as is signified in the Scripture, according to the interpretation of the Apostle, when it says [1 Cor. 9:9], "Thou shalt not muzzle the ox that treadeth out the corn." [II, x, 15]

The trope is defined here as a symbolism of objects that is transmitted by language. The sentence about the ox, attributed in Deuteronomy to God, is interpreted by Saint Paul in the First Epistle to the Corinthians as having to do with those who announce the Gospel. But the words themselves do not change meaning; it is the object—the ox—which, in a second phase, evokes the Evangelist.

However, one page later, Augustine cites another example of a transposed sign. He comments as follows on the sentence of the prophet Isaiah "Despise not the family of thy seed" (Isa. 58:7): "The 'family of the seed' may be taken figuratively so that it is understood to mean 'Christians' born spiritually from the seed of the Word which produced us" (II, xii, 17). Here we no longer find a symbolism of objects: the words used are to be taken in a different sense, as is the case with rhetorical tropes.

[2]Trans. D. W. Robertson, Jr. (Indianapolis, 1958). All quotations from *On Christian Doctrine* are from this edition, abbreviated *OCD*.

42

These two divergent examples do not bear witness to some confusion in Augustine's mind, but rather to his desire to broaden the category of the "transposed." We no longer have two descriptions of a single phenomenon, but a subdivision within it. The opposition is formulated still more sharply in *On the Trinity,* in which Augustine comments on the allegorical interpretation proposed by Saint Paul of the two wives and two sons of Abraham, as the worldly and heavenly Jerusalems (Gal. 4:22):

> But when the apostle spoke of an allegory, he does not find it in the words, but in the fact; since he has shown that the two Testaments are to be understood by the two sons of Abraham, one by a bondmaid and the other by a free woman, which was a thing not only said but also done. [xv, 9, 15][3]

This formula is at the root of one of the most important distinctions in Christian hermeneutics, the one between *allegoria in factis* and *allegoria in verbis.* "Allegory" here designates the whole of the symbolic; "factual" (or "real") and "verbal" allegories are its species.

The examples quoted make it clear that we are dealing with phenomena identical to those I discussed earlier in connection with lexical and propositional symbolism. I could have said that "animals" understood in the sense of *meek men* involved a change in the meaning of the words; and that in the other instance, on the contrary, the thing evoked (the animals' reward) in itself allowed us to deduce a new meaning (concerning men's reward). Which of these two descriptions is preferable?

The problem with the opposition between verbal and real allegory is not only that it is a substantive one and does not reveal the mechanism that produces the different phenomena. There is another problem as well: the tropes (= verbal allegory) are just as "real" as the real allegories themselves.

[3]In *Basic Writings,* trans. Whitney J. Oates (New York, 1948), vol. 2.

If I say "the ox" in order to designate a dull man meta-phorically (this is not what Saint Paul was suggesting), I have to refer to the animal itself, in order to find some resemblance between it and this sort of man. In this respect, the case is no different from the one in which the words indeed designate the ox but where the ox in turn evokes the Evangelist. The word/thing opposition used here is a somewhat awkward way of referring to the fact that the meaning of the initial statement is maintained in one case, abolished in the other. In "verbal allegory" the statement concerning the animal disappears; in "real allegory" it remains. This fact itself is revealed in the linguistic difference between the segments that serve as point of departure for interpretation: word or proposition.

It is just the same with Abraham's two wives. If for example "wives" were used to mean *weaknesses,* it would not be a case of forgetting the thing itself, but of abolishing the initial statement: nothing would have been said about Abraham's (literal) wives. Saint Paul interprets the sentence differently: Abraham indeed has two wives (the meaning of the initial statement is preserved), but these wives prefigure the two Jerusalems. Here as before we cross through the world of "things": only the status of the initial statement varies.

The same remarks hold true for a somewhat different formulation of the same opposition, found in Thomas Aquinas. The opposition is more pronounced here, for whereas Augustine recognizes that any form of symbolism may be found in the Bible, Aquinas leaves lexical symbolism to the poets and claims as a mode of divine expression only (one form of) propositional symbolism. Starting from the same *factis/verbis* opposition, he stresses that one of the interpretations is successive, the other simultaneous.

These various readings do not set up ambiguity or any other kind of mixture of meanings, because, as we have explained, they are many, not because one term may signify many things, but because the things signified by the terms can themselves be the signs of other things . . . . The parabolic sense [synonymous with verbal allegory, the kind that men too can use] is contained in the literal sense, for words can signify something properly and something figuratively; in the last case the literal sense is not the figure of speech itself, but the object it figures. When Scripture speaks of the arm of God, the literal sense is not that he has a physical limb, but that he has what it signifies, namely the power of doing and making.[4]

We shall not be concerned here with the divisions between proper meaning, transposed meaning, literal meaning, and spiritual meaning, which differ in Augustine and Aquinas. It remains the case that in "real allegory" it is necessary, according to Thomas, *first* to interpret the words, *next* the things that these words designate; whereas in "verbal allegory" (or parables) the two meanings are given simultaneously. But here again only one of the descriptions is precise. To return to our initial example, it is true that it is necessary first to understand the sentence "animals will be rewarded" in order to deduce from it, subsequently, that men will be rewarded also. But the same holds true in the other instance: we understand the meaning *animal* first, and only afterward that of *meek;* it is through the initial meaning *animal* that we reach the second meaning *men;* that is a property of all indirect meaning. And, whatever Aquinas might say, when we hear someone's arm mentioned we first think of an *arm,* and only in a second stage, having decided that this first meaning is unacceptable, do we pass from *arm* to *power of doing and making.* At the same time, we see perfectly well what Aquinas had in mind: in one case, we understand the first proposition, then add a second one to it; in the other case, we conceive of a first interpretation, then *substitute* another for it. But this dif-

[4]*Summa Theologiae* (New York, 1964–76), vol. 1.

ference clearly stems from the fate in store for the initial statement, which is in the one case preserved, in the other abolished. In the case of tropes, meaning is also added; but it is the meaning of a word and not of a proposition. In short, the process is the same in both cases: if there are different results, it is because the process is applied to different entities, words and propositions.

Quintilian touches on the same problem in his rhetoric, without stating it in explicit terms. He contrasts tropes and figures, but he does not take a position on the categories that underlie the opposition between words (tropes) and propositions (figures) or between form (figures) and meaning (tropes); hence the awkward tripartite division into tropes / word figures / thought figures. It is because of this that irony appears both as a subdivision of allegory (and thus as a trope) and as a thought figure. Quintilian attempts to reconcile these positions as follows: "Thus, as continued metaphor develops into allegory, so a sustained metaphor develops into this figure [irony]" (*Institutio Oratoria*, ix, 2, 46).[5] But if allegory is opposed to metaphor as figure is opposed to trope, then allegory is no longer a trope? Another indication leads in the same direction: the *example* is presented as a subdivision of allegory; now, as Quintilian's illustrations demonstrate, the *example* derives from propositional, not lexical, symbolism (the same is true for the *proverb,* similarly indexed); but the cases of allegory take the opposite course: allegory is nothing but the accumulation of several metaphors drawn from the same area:

> "O ship, new waves will bear thee back to sea. What dost thou? Make the haven, come what may," and the rest of the ode, in which Horace represents the state under the semblance of a ship, the civil wars as tempests, and peace and good-will as the haven. [viii, 6, 44]

[5]Trans. H. E. Butler (New York: Loeb Classical Library, 1921).

As Quintilian's commentary shows, we are dealing here with several words (metaphors) and not with a proposition: there is no sustained statement regarding a real ship that would allow us, in a second stage, to compare it to the state. The extended metaphor is nonetheless a metaphor; it does not belong to propositional symbolism. The latter is not explicitly recognized in the *Institutio Oratoria*.

Absent from Western works of rhetoric or hermeneutics in this specific form, the distinction between lexical and propositional symbolism seems to occur in the Sanskrit tradition. The phenomena that interest us here were first described separately, before anyone sought to characterize their articulation. The first to embrace the entire field seems to have been once again Ānandavardhana, author of the theory of *dhvani;* and his commentator Abhinavagupta is quite explicit on this point:

> Abhinavagupta speaks of four distinct functions of words, *abhidhā, tātparya, lakṣaṇa* and *vyañjanā*, and arranges them under four separate classes: *abhidhā* is the power of the words to signify the primary meaning; this primary meaning refers only to the universal and not to the particular. In a sentence the individual words by their primary definition of *abhidhā* refer only to the isolated word-meanings. The syntactic relation of these is conveyed by the *tātparyaśakti* of the words. The intention of the speaker, or the general purport of the utterance, is obviously to give a unified purposeful sentence-meaning. Hence the words are considered to have a power to convey the syntactic relation among the various isolated word-meanings. This power is called *tātparyaśakti*. *Lakṣaṇā* is the third power recognized according to this theory; it is accepted only when the primary meanings cannot be syntactically connected to give a meaning. Abhinavagupta says that even according to this theory *vyañjanā* or suggestion will have to be accepted as the fourth function of words. [In Kunjunni Raja, pp. 213–214]

Thus of the four types of signification, two are direct (*abhidhā* and *tātparya*) and two are indirect (*lakṣaṇā* and *vyañjanā*). The first two terms are opposed to each other, moreover, as the word is to the proposition. We may thus assume that the opposition between the two indirect forms is of the same nature. This is indeed what Ānandavardhana seems to have had in mind in his discussion of the *lakṣaṇā-vyañjanā* relationship. For he states that in the former case the meaning of the initial proposition is abolished, whereas in the latter case it is maintained: *"Lakṣaṇā* operates when there is some kind of inconsistency in the primary sense; it indicates the secondary metaphorical sense after cancelling its primary sense; but in suggestion the primary sense need not be discarded" (p. 296).

Furthermore, the difference between *tātparya* and *vyañjanā* lies only in the direct/indirect option; thus both stem from the proposition.

> Abhinavagupta says that when an expression gives its own literal meaning, and in addition suggests some other sense, we cannot regard both these distinct senses as conveyed by the same power. The former proceeds directly from the words, while the latter comes from this literal sense. [Pp. 301–302]

My insistence on separating these two types of symbolism according to whether the meaning of the initial statement is maintained or abolished might set this distinction alongside another one that is also found in Sanskrit poetics. According to these texts, two types of tropes can be identified: those in which the first meaning must be abandoned in order for the second to be recognized; and those in which the second meaning is added to the first without eradicating it; in other words, the two statements, literal and tropic, may be compatible or incompatible, inclusive or exclusive. An example of the first type will be metonymy: there is no village *on* the Ganges (even though we speak in such terms), but only on the banks of the Ganges. (Metaphor belongs to the same class.) The second case can be illustrated by synecdoche: "The lances came into the room" (instead of "the lancers") is not a false statement, but it describes only a part of the fact, the rest being simply evoked by the trope. (The same would hold true for litotes.) Is the difference between lexical and propositional symbolism reduced then to the difference between metaphor and synecdoche? It suffices to compare the examples of propositional symbolism and synecdoche given above to realize the importance of the differences. In the case of synecdoche, we have two descriptions of the *same fact* (the entrance of the lancers); one of the statements describes the fact more completely than the other. In propositional symbolism, on the other hand, from the first proposition we deduce not a better description of the same fact but the description of a *second fact:* from the fact that animals will be rewarded we conclude that men will be rewarded too. Thus this new distinction made by the Sanskrit poeticians, a very useful one in itself, does not coincide with mine.

Symbolism of the Signifier

In distributing symbolic phenomena, in the present context, into just two groups, according to whether the initial statement is maintained or not, and consequently, according to whether the association starts with a proposition or a word, I am leaving no room within verbal symbolism for those well-known phenomena called *phonetic symbolism* or *graphic symbolism*. This is not by accident. One of two things must be true: either such symbolism is independent of the meaning of the words, and then we are in the infralinguistic and not the verbal realm (these phenomena stem from aural or visual symbolism; for example, *i* evokes smallness); or else this symbolism implies the meaning of the words, but then it only parallels an indispensable semantic motivation, as when Charles Nodier claims that the word catacomb (Fr. *catacombe*) phonetically symbolizes coffin, subterranean, cataract and tomb (Fr. *cerceuil, souterrain, cataracte, tombe*). (I shall return to

49

this point in the chapter on logical structure.) This is why the study of these problems is not appropriate here; I shall do no more than refer to a summary treatment of the question (see the bibliography).

Other Effects of Linguistic Structure

Let us note, finally, that the overall distribution that I have proposed is far from being the only point on which linguistic structure determines the symbolic interpretation. Let us compare the following sentences:

(1) You know that tonight there is a green crime to commit (*Magnetic Fields*).
(2) You know that tonight there is a green crime in the room next door.

The need for interpretation is signaled in each instance by an incompatibility within the sentence (a semantic anomaly): the impossible combination is "green crime." But in the first case it is "green" which becomes the starting point for associations (the term is interpreted metaphorically), whereas in the second sentence, owing to the adverbial complement of place, things change, and it is not certain that the interpreter will not start rather with "crime," by interpreting it metonymically (for example as "result of crime").

Let us take these other two sentences:

(1) That man is a lion.
(2) That lion is a man.

Each time, it is the predicate that supplies the starting point for associations. But the motivation evoked in the first case (let us say, "courage") will not be the same as in the second (rather, "intelligence").

Such facts—and they are numerous—attest to the pertinence of syntactic structures for the form taken by symbolic interpretation. But they belong to linguistics (to semantics) rather than to symbolics, and I must content myself here with urging that they be studied in the appropriate framework.

The Hierarchy of Meanings

The very terms currently used to designate direct and indirect meanings reveal a hierarchy—one that the user of the terms does not always recognize. We have already seen how the expression "metaphorical meaning" is misleading: it inclines us to think that the word has *changed* meaning, and that the new meaning has simply displaced the old. Things are no better if we follow I. A. Richards and call the first meaning "vehicle" and the second "tenor": even though he is opposed to the substitution theory of metaphor, Richards maintains a rigid hierarchy here, since direct meaning is nothing but an instrument for indirect, and does not have "tenor" in itself. But while the two meanings (and often more than two) do indeed remain present, and while they do differ as to their hierarchical position, they are no different in nature. Nor can one speak here of "manifest meaning" and "latent meaning," for both of these are perfectly accessible to conscious perception. "Denotation" and "connotation" are somewhat better, but these terms too can lead to the error which would hold that the two meanings are different in nature, whereas the operations by which they are produced, designated by two related terms, are practically identical. Precisely the opposite is true: the nature of the meanings is identical in both cases; only their mode of existence differs.

In an attempt to stake out the problematics of hierarchy,

52

one might first establish the respective positions of the particularly clear cases that I will call literal discourse, ambiguous discourse, and transparent discourse.

Literal Discourse

Literal discourse is discourse that signifies without evoking anything. Obviously we have a limit here that probably no actual text embodies; it is important, however, to conceive of it, for it constitutes one of the magnetic poles of writing, and may be claimed by any literary movement. The earliest theoreticians of the New Novel, for instance, challenging the previous overvalorization of the metaphorical, insisted on a perfectly literal reading for these new works. Alain Robbe-Grillet wrote, in a programmatic text:

> The world is neither significant nor absurd. It *is*, quite simply.
> . . . Instead of this universe of "signification" (psychological, social, functional), we must try, then, to construct a world both more solid and more immediate. Let it be first of all by their *presence* that objects and and gestures continue to prevail. [1]

Naturally—as their later critical history has amply demonstrated—these new novels were not innocent of all symbolic evocation; the claim made for them functioned nonetheless as an indication of genre, and was able to produce, if not literal texts, at least literal readings.

Indeed, even the most literal utterance inevitably evokes a group of other meanings. Aristotle, writing in the *Topics*, understood this perfectly:

> Any one who has made any statement whatever has in a certain sense made several statements, inasmuch as each statement has a number of necessary consequences: e.g. the man who

[1] *For a New Novel*, trans. Richard Howard (New York, 1965), pp. 19–21.

53

said "X is a man" has also said that it is an animal and a biped and capable of acquiring reason and knowledge (112a).[2]

In our day, William Empson has taught us to see that words are "complex," and linguistics has emphasized the phenomenon of presupposition, the linguistic meaning borne implicitly by each sentence. Literal discourse is not discourse from which any secondary meaning would be absent, but discourse in which secondary meanings are completely subordinate to the direct meaning. Every word is complex and every sentence is charged with presuppositions, but we do not grasp that complexity unless our attention is somehow drawn to it. Jokes can do this:

"Is this the place where the Duke of Wellington spoke those words?"
"Yes, it is the place, but he never spoke the words."

To say that "X did p at N" presupposes that "X did something at N" and that "Someone did p at N" and that "X did p somewhere": thus one cannot accept the global statement while denying this presupposition—unless we are making a joke. Through this technique, what was only a subordinate meaning relegated to the background comes to the center of our attention.

Ambiguous Discourse

Discourse is ambiguous when several meanings of the same utterance are to be taken on exactly the same level. The ambiguity may be syntactic (the same sentence refers to two different underlying structures), semantic (the sentence includes polysemic words), or pragmatic (the sentence is a po-

[2]Aristotle is quoted from the *Works of Aristotle* translated into English under the editorship of W. D. Ross, 12 vols. (Oxford, 1908–1952).

tential bearer of several illocutionary values): the ambiguity is never symbolic in itself, since all the meanings are direct, and are signified by the signifier, without any one of them being signified by a primary signified. This was well understood by the Sanskrit poeticians who distinguished clearly between *dhvani* (suggestion) and *çleṣa* (coalescence).

It is possible nevertheless to obtain symbolic effects on the basis of ambiguity: even though they are all direct, the meanings of a word or of a sentence may be arranged hierarchically (this may be on the semantic, syntactic, or pragmatic level). One of them comes to mind first, and it is only in a second stage that we discover that we should in fact have been thinking of the other. In this connection William Empson uses the terms "head meaning" for the meaning which "holds a more or less permanent position as the first one in its structure" and "chief meaning" for the meaning "which the user feels to be the first one in play at the moment" (p. 38). When, in the interpretation of an utterance, one moves from the head meaning, which has come to mind first, to the chief meaning, a phenomenon occurs that is very similar (but not identical) to symbolic evocation; I shall return to this in the next chapter. Once again we find that jokes exploit misunderstanding in the comprehension of ambiguous sentences. For example:

Two Jews met in the neighborhood of the bath-house. "Have you taken a bath?" asked one of them. "What?" asked the other in return, "is there one missing?"

The head meaning (because it is the idiomatic meaning) of "taking a bath" is *to bathe;* but in retrospect the expression may be taken literally, as *to take away a bath(tub).* Still, this reminder contrasts with the properly symbolic evocation, illustrated here by the response of the second speaker. From the fact that he thinks of this implausible meaning, we deduce the anti-Semitic flavor of the joke: Jews do not bathe, and are preoccupied with acquisition.

Transparent Discourse

Finally, discourse is transparent if when we perceive it we pay no attention to its literal meaning (since the romantic era the term "allegory" has sometimes been used to designate this type of utterance). Moralist plays and fables sometimes come close to this ideal. Euphemisms provide a striking example. All members of a society know the real meaning of a euphemism; if it is not to become useless and thus unusable, it is nevertheless necessary that the presence of the literal meaning be attested, however tenuous it may be. One step further and we find ourselves among the "dead metaphors" which, in synchrony, stem from polysemy and not symbolism.

Intermediate Cases

These three extreme and relatively clear cases—literality, ambiguity, transparency—are also the only ones that we are really able to identify; but they obviously constitute only the limits of a field in which numerous intermediate cases can be found. We note these latter cases intuitively, I think, but are unable to name them, still less to analyze them. This is no accident: our rhetorics, the richest catalogue available to the Western tradition dealing with symbolic phenomena, see resemblance as a simple and unanalyzable relation. This is not the situation, once again, for Sanskrit poetics, which is able to identify as many as one hundred twenty varieties of comparison—and which, in any case, possesses quite distinct categories with which to say that the comparing term imposes its meaning on the compared term, or vice versa; that the two are identical or are only copresent; that their assimilation is produced objectively or in the eyes of a single observer. I can thus do no more than deplore the absence of instruments that would allow us to analyze the hierarchy of meanings in symbolic evocation and must content myself with illustrating the variety of hierarchical relations by means of one or two examples (I have already done this in *The Fantastic: A Structural Approach to a Literary Genre.*[3])

I shall begin with two paragraphs from the beginning of the *Legend of Saint Julian the Hospitaller.*

> In the courtyard, the stone flagging was as immaculate as the floor of a church. Long rain-spouts, representing dragons with yawning jaws, directed the water towards the cistern, and on each window-sill of the castle a basil or a heliotrope bush bloomed, in painted flower-pots.[4]

Here is a description that might be considered perfectly literal; so it is, at least at this point in the narrative (I shall return later to the secondary effect of the comparison "as... a church").

But a few lines later, we read this other paragraph, at first glance entirely comparable:

> Peace had reigned so long that the portcullis was never lowered; the moats were filled with water; swallows built their nests in the cracks of the battlements, and as soon as the sun shone too strongly, the archer who all day long paced to and fro on the curtain, withdrew to the watch-tower and slept soundly.

Once again a literal description? No, for it happens to be introduced by the proposition "peace had reigned so long that...," which changes the status of all that follows: here we have only illustrations, examples of that eternal peace, four details by means of which, as usual, Flaubert communicates to us some general information. The landscape, the castle, its specific features are not described simply so that they may "be there," as Robbe-Grillet would have said, but in order to

---

[3]Trans. Richard Howard (Ithaca, 1975).
[4]*The Works of Gustave Flaubert* (New York, 1904), p. 287.

illustrate an abstract statement. A statement which happens, moreover, to be formulated explicitly here, and which thus does not belong to the symbolic; but its relation with what follows imposes upon the reader a way of interpreting—and it may oblige him to return to the paragraph first quoted, in order to ask himself whether that initial description was as literal as it appeared, or whether it was not there to illustrate another general statement, not concerning peace in that case but, let us say, the perfection of the site.

Now let us take two examples from Baudelaire's *Little Poems in Prose*. A text entitled "Already!" relates the experience of someone who was approaching land at the end of a long sea voyage; all the details, all the anecdotes relate to a specific voyage. Then there is a comparison:

> Like a priest whose God has been snatched from him, I could not without heartbreaking bitterness tear myself away from the sea, so monotonously seductive, so infinitely varied in her terrible simplicity and seeming to contain and to represent by all her changing moods, the angers, smiles, humors, agonies and ecstasies of all the souls who have lived, who live, or who will some day live![5]

The material and actual sea of the preceding paragraphs is effaced little by little: first it is qualified by terms that integrate it into the animate world (seduction, simplicity), then, after the fleeting desire to make of it a metonymy for life has appeared ("to contain"), it is transformed into a transparent allegory, explicitly introduced by the verb "to represent," for all feelings of all beings. But, having read that sentence, do we not retrace our steps to ask ourselves what was symbolized by each aspect of the sea described earlier, each of the episodes in which it figured? Since the sea is only the allegory of life, everything must be reinterpreted? And yet, no, the sea

[5] *Paris Spleen*, trans. Louise Varèse (New York, 1970), pp. 75–76.

of the beginning is really the sea, even if here it has become perfectly "transparent."

Much the same thing happens in "Evening Twilight." Here again, we begin with a concrete description of a certain hour of the day, then we follow a series of related anecdotes. But, toward the end, the chief comparison comes once more:

> The rosy glow lingering on the horizon like the last agony of day conquered by victorious night; the flames of the candelabra making dull red splashes against the sunset's dying glory; the heavy draperies that some unseen hand draws out of the depth of the East—it all seems to imitate those complex sentiments that at life's most solemn moments war with each other in man's heart. [P. 45]

The description of the literal sunset (even though it is amply metaphorical) gives way at a certain point to the "transparent" evocation of "those complex sentiments": the passage is marked explicitly this time by the verb "imitate." Once more this revelation obliges us to reinterpret all that precedes in allegorical terms—and yet it does not entirely efface the literal description of the sunset.

It is evident that Flaubert's approach and Baudelaire's are different (the narrative and the poetic are contrasted here, and not merely two personalities, contemporaries though they be); however, in neither case do we have pure literality, nor transparency, nor ambiguity. But this negative demarcation is obviously inadequate, and fails to account for the complexity of the hierarchical relations of meanings—a complexity that I have had here to evoke rather than to designate.

The Direction of Evocation

Symbolic evocation is profoundly multiple. Literary translators know this all too well, for they must attempt to transpose into another language not only the direct meaning of a sentence, but also its various symbolic resonances. The difficulty arises precisely from the multiplicity of these resonances, for if one of them is pursued another is lost. How is it possible to maintain at one and the same time semantic precision, phonic resemblance, intertextual evocation, implications concerning the speaker, and much more?

In this chapter I should like to review once again some of the possible subdivisions of the symbolic realm: those that arise, in this case, from the interlocutors' choice of the very *direction* in which the evocation is made to function.

Utterance and Enunciation

A first rough categorization comes from the fact that the devices of symbolic evocation may be "based upon *the content of the utterance*" or else may "involve the *fact of the enunciation*" (Oswald Ducrot). The difference is radical: in the first case, the interlocutor starts with the object of the utterance and adds to it a content of the same order; in the second, the utterance is perceived as an action, not as a means of transmitting information, and the implication concerns the speaker, the subject and not the object.

A passage from Henry James (*The Awkward Age*) illustrates these two forms of evocation nicely. In his conversation with Mr. Longdon, Vanderbank states that Mrs. Brook has for several years been making her daughter out to be younger than she really is. Mr. Longdon understands the implication of the utterance perfectly well: namely, that Mrs. Brook herself is trying to appear younger than her years. But he does not stop there: what strikes him in the sentence in question is that Vanderbank was able to produce it, that is, that he allows himself to speak ill of his friends in their absence. Mr. Longdon's interpretation of this utterance thus amounts, or almost, to a criticism of its originator: "You are a vulgar creature." The distribution of the symbolism here between utterance and enunciation coincides with another distinction between voluntary and involuntary, or even between conscious and unconscious. But such a distribution is not obligatory. Obviously, one may aim to produce implications concerning the enunciation in a perfectly conscious way: I use incomprehensible words so that I will be seen as erudite, for example.

In fact, an implication concerning the enunciation is necessarily present in any symbolic evocation (this will oblige us to complete the image of the interpretive process evoked at the beginning of this discussion). Indeed, in order to arrive at the implication concerning the utterance ("Mrs Brook is trying to appear younger than her years"), Mr. Longdon must first have said to himself that the utterance according to which Mrs. Brook is making her daughter out to be younger than she really is does not satisfy the principle of pertinence, if it means only what it signifies; but, *knowing Vanderbank* (and it is here that reference is made to the enunciation), I presume that this utterance means something more, namely, that Mrs.

Brook is trying to appear younger than she is. The reference to the enunciation is thus already present; but it may play a dominant role or a subordinate one, as in this first case; and it may then be put provisionally aside, so that the implications concerning the utterance and those concerning the enunciation may be contrasted.

Irony

The complex phenomenon of irony may be clarified in the light of these distinctions. Irony plays simultaneously upon the utterance and the enunciation, more or less, as the case may be; descriptions of irony have ordinarily preserved only one of these aspects. Let us take two examples. If I say: "What lovely weather!" whereas it is raining cats and dogs, I mean—as rhetoricians have been telling us since ancient times—the opposite of what I am saying: what rotten weather! But in order to understand this, the interlocutor has had to grasp an implication concerning the enunciation and concerning me as well: to note the irony, he has first had to recognize that I knew the meaning of the words, and that I was in my right mind.

Now let us take this other sentence: "The Penguins had the best army in the world. So did the Porpoises" (Anatole France). Here I am no longer attempting to say the opposite of what I am saying, as the rhetoricians would have it. If I replace "best" by its opposite, "worst," proceeding as I did in the earlier example, I do not obtain the indirect and nonironic meaning of my initial utterance: I obtain a new ironic utterance, exactly as ironic as the first one. The implication here concerns the enunciation: the absurdity of the initial utterance implies that the speaking subject does not assume his utterance, he is rather imitating some other utterance (for example that of the Penguins and that of the Porpoises, made independently of each other). The irony is translatable in this instance not by substituting one term for its opposite, but by including the utterance in another utterance: "I am not saying that p", and thus "Certain people (but not I) would say that p"; the irony is equivalent here to a (pseudo) quotation, to a parenthetical aside (Dan Sperber). However, in this case of stress on the enunciation, the implication concerning the utterance is not totally absent either: I do mean, in fact, that the Penguin army is *not* the best in the world, any more than the Porpoise army is. In the two examples, therefore, the evocation is double, concerning both the utterance and the enunciation; but in what might be called antiphrasis-irony, the stress falls on the inversion of the content of the utterance; whereas in quotation-irony, it concerns the inauthenticity of the initial act of enunciation.

Hyperbole and litotes are based on a similar mechanism. When someone says "For me, eternity will be but an instant," the listener understands both that eternity will appear brief (association concerning the utterance, implying exaggeration) and that the speaker is placing particular stress upon what he is saying (association concerning the enunciation). Chimène's famous line "Go, I do not hate you" (*Le Cid*, III, iv) will be interpreted both as a diminished designation of the sentiment in question, and as a proof of the speaker's self-control. The two associations always imply each other mutually, but one or the other may be stressed.

Intertextuality

A second major difference in the direction of evocation, which makes it possible to distinguish among symbolic phenomena, comes from the fact that the evocation may or may not point toward another text, which it locates, so to speak, in the signifier or in the signified.

The association may indeed lead to other words, taken in their phonetic, morphological, or stylistic specificity; these phenomena have been called *intertextuality* in the recent literature; and they themselves are extremely varied. I shall do no more here than enumerate the major principles underlying this variety. One of them is quantitative: one text may evoke a single other text, as *Jacques le fataliste* plays with *Tristram Shandy;* or an entire genre, as *Don Quixote* does for novels of knighthood; or a particular milieu, as when a slang phrase evokes the milieu where the slang prevails; or an entire epoch, as *Madame Bovary* does for the romantic period. The other principle is qualitative: the evocation may go from condemnation (as is usually the case with parodies) to praise (implied by imitation and stylization).

Two more general remarks will complete this rapid review. The first is that intertextual phenomena are located at the frontier of the symbolic realm, and sometimes move outside it. For not every evocation of something absent is symbolic. There are certainly cases in which association with another text is precisely the meaning that the given linguistic segment is intended to transmit; but there are others in which this association functions rather as a condition for the constitution of the meaning of the utterance given, without at any moment becoming that meaning itself. *Tristram Shandy* is not the indirect meaning of *Jacques le fataliste*, but the relation between the two is necessary to establish the meaning, direct and indirect, of the latter novel. Alongside these symbolic evocations, there exist others, then, whose function is above all to contribute to the formation of a configuration, and which could for that reason be called figural relations.

The second remark has to do with the limits that make it possible to circumscribe the intertextual phenomenon itself: a phenomenon whose existence is threatened by its omnipresence. Whatever Montaigne may say, there is no such thing as a private language; words belong to everyone. Consequently, as soon as one engages in verbal activity, one evokes previous discourses—through the very fact that one is using the same words, the same grammar. It is probable that if we were to sift carefully through all the publications that immediately preceded the *Fleurs du mal*, we would find not only all the words Baudelaire used—that goes without saying—but even all his phrases; and it is well known that source criticism has managed to establish such juxtapositions. But by virtue of seeing intertextuality everywhere, one loses the means of identifying and distinguishing the texts where it plays a constitutive role. Thus the global principle of the necessary presence of an intertextual dimension must be moderated and nuanced by appropriate rules, which make it possible to distinguish the cases where intertextuality is pertinent from those where it is not.

Extratextual, Intratextual

A third way of distinguishing among symbolic phenomena according to the direction of evocation consists in asking whether the indirect meaning concerns the text that is the starting point or whether it is external to this text, instead; it consists, then, in separating intratextual and extratextual symbolism (in *S/Z*, Barthes calls the former the semic code and the latter the symbolic code).

This latter case needs no commentary: the Faustian trajectory symbolizes the destiny of humanity, as Don Juan's symbolizes the vicissitudes of the love relationship; these "destinations" are not internal to Goethe's text or Molière's. On the other hand, when an old sailor tosses a knot of ropes into Captain Delano's hands in Melville's *Benito Cereno*, the knot symbolizes nothing other than the problem which is confronting the captain at that very moment: Delano remains on deck, "knot in hand, and knot in head," as Melville writes.

Intratextual symbolism is chiefly responsible for the way in which character and thought (to take two Aristotelian categories) are constructed within a fiction. The author has at his disposal two ways to construct his characters: by naming their attributes directly, or by leaving the reader with the task of deducing these attributes on the basis of what the characters say and do. Through the ages literature has favored sometimes the one mode of presentation, sometimes the other. The same thing is true for the communication of general ideas: Constant or Proust can easily conclude a paragraph with a sentence that is sharply differentiated from what precedes, written in the atemporal present and preceded by a universal quantifier. But other writers forswear any formulation of pronouncements and yet continue nonetheless to transmit general ideas: they do so by inciting the reader to deduce them from the actions that make up the book's plot. Such are the cases in which the "destination" of symbolic evocation lies within the text itself.

As in the case of intertextual relations, a place must be reserved here for intratextual relations that are not symbolic but figural. The fact that each chapter of a short story may be longer (or shorter) than the preceding one may introduce into the narrative a gradation and a rhythm necessary to the interpretation of the chapter; but this does not mean that one chapter symbolizes another.

Contexts: Paradigmatic and Syntagmatic

I shall introduce here a fourth and final distinction that involves not the direction of the evocation itself, but the nature of the means that make it possible to establish the indirect meaning (whether in its production or its reception). Once again I shall apply a distinction previously introduced on the occasion of the discussion of the indices leading to interpretation: the distinction between reference to the immediate syntagmatic context and recourse to collective memory, to knowledge shared by the members of a society (this seems to be the point of Schleiermacher's famous distinction between *technical* and *grammatical* interpretation; see below, p. 157).

Symbolism based on collective memory is the one that countless dictionaries of symbols, whatever their inspiration and ambition, seek to catalogue. It is also an indispensable tool for religious or psychoanalytic interpretations: each of these exegetic strategies possesses its own "vocabulary," preestablished lists of equivalences which allow it to substitute a meaning for an image more or less automatically. Similarly, there are esoteric readings (alchemist, astrological, and so on) to which any text may be subjected, and from which often surprising results may be obtained. So-called "internal" literary criticism, as we know, specifically refuses any recourse to "shortcuts" of this type: if the number three has to symbolize something, it is not because "three" evokes this or that in the readers' collective memory, but because it appears in certain specific contexts, within the very work that is being interpreted.

In practice, we constantly call upon both registers. When Mr. Longdon interpreted "she is making her daughter out to be younger than she really is" by "therefore she herself wants to appear younger than her years," he had to call upon a commonplace notion of his own society, according to which one of these actions always has the other as its goal. In this connection, let us note the nature of such commonplace notions, and, consequently, the way in which collective memory is presented. If we were to ask someone to list the rules of the society to which he belongs, he would certainly not think of the one that authorizes the present inference. However, it sufficed for one character to utter the first sentence, or something like it, for Mr. Longdon, and with him the readers of the novel, to grasp the unstated, "understood" notion, which implies the presence of this connection in their minds. The fact is that collective memory is passive: its content is summoned up only owing to the focalization brought about by the sentence produced. Commonplaces are not so much present as *available* in everyone's memory. As for inferences, they of course do not conform to the strict rules of formal logic; they correspond to what Aristotle called "enthymemes," or rhetorical syllogisms, which lead toward plausibility rather than to truth.

On the other hand, when Mr. Longdon says in effect to his companion on another occasion: your mother liked me more than the others did, and Vanderbank interprets: you mean that you loved her without being loved in return, he does it by referring not to collective memory but to the immediate context. In the preceding sentences Mr. Longdon himself has established the connection between these two facts: the women he loved were content to respond with "the dreadful consolatory 'liking.' "

It is this possibility of reference to two different frameworks (syntagmatic context or collective memory) which allows us to understand a mechanism evoked in the preceding chapter, that of the replacement of the "head meaning" by the "chief meaning": jokes often play upon the possibility of evoking two *different* meanings of a word at the same time, owing to this double reference. For example:

> "How are you coming along?" said the blind man to the cripple.
> "Just as you see," replied the cripple to the blind man.

Collective memory (here a properly linguistic one) brings to mind the current (thus head) meaning of the expressions "how are you coming along" and "as you see." The immediate syntagmatic context (the words "blind," "paralytic") awakens the literal meaning of the elements constituting these expressions (come, see).

The important difference between these two forms of symbolic evocation is that in the one case the shared knowledge necessary to interpretation has to be uttered explicitly, and thus assumed by its speakers, whereas the implicit reference characteristic of the other imposes *complicity* on the interlocutors. It is because they have a common collective memory and belong to the same social group that they can understand each other. The affirmation of this complicity may even be the only real goal of such an indirect evocation; moreover, this constitutes an excellent way to gain acceptance for an assertion without having to formulate it and thus subject it to the critical attention of the interlocutors, as every specialist of persuasion and demagogy knows. Refusing to understand is the only way to reject this complicity (as when I refuse to recognize racist jokes by laughing at them, and thus refuse to understand them).

Logical Structure

Perhaps the most debated aspect of the symbolic process is the relation between direct and indirect meanings. Given these two comparable entities, how can we describe the relation that holds between them? Speaking schematically, one might say that two types of answers have been proposed. One type of description seeks to model symbolic relations on what is known of discursive relations; the other describes the symbolic in some particular way without attempting to relate it to other associations that are seen as operative in language.

Global Taxonomies

The first approach has been with us since ancient times, but one cannot say that it has been systematically explored. At the beginning of this discussion I mentioned the possible relationships among Aristotle's various classifications, as well as the theory of accessory ideas in Port-Royal's *Logic* and its heirs. The Stoics called propositional inference "sign," and the Indian logician Mahimabhaṭṭale argued, against the theoreticians of *dhvani* (suggestion), that the latter is only a special case of inference. We can recall, too, that Quintilian defined metaphor (symbolic relation) as condensed comparison (discursive relation). In the late nineteenth century, the Russian linguist A. A. Potebnia pushed the parallelism fur-

ther: he put synecdoche and epithet on the same plane, pre-
serving only the difference between implicit and explicit, and
broadening Quintilian's formula as follows:

> Every completed naming provides us with the comparison of
> two mental complexes: signifier and signified [Potebnia is thus
> identifying the subject-predicate pair with the signifier-
> signified pair]. When both entities are expressed verbally, the
> relationship between the two may be synecdochic as well as
> metonymic or metaphoric.[1]

The symbolic can henceforth be described with the same
degree of subtlety as discursive relations. In *The Structure of
Complex Words*, Empson postulates (p. 41) that the relationship between direct and indirect meaning can be translated
by the predication formula "*A* is *B*," where *A* and *B* are two
meanings of a word; and he goes on to spell out four semantic
variants of this elementary proposition: "*A* is part of *B*," "*A*
entails *B*," "*A* is like *B*," and, a somewhat special case, "*A* is
typical of *B*." This corresponds quite well to the traditional rhetorical subdivision into synecdoche (belonging), metonymy (causality), and metaphor (comparison, resemblance).
If, for the discursive realm, one started with grammatical
categories instead, one would have a description of the symbolic that cannot be reproduced within the traditional categories of rhetoric: possession would give rise to the genitive
and to synecdoche, apposition and attribution would be
linked with metaphor (which also has certain relations
with coordination); but metonymy would mix causal (transi-
tive, accusative), instrumental, and circumstantial (locative)
relations, and it is hard to see what trope would correspond
to the dative. If, on the other hand, one were to go along
with Charles Bally in reducing discursive relations to two
and only two, inherence and copenetration on the one hand,

---

[1]Aleksandr A. Potebnia, *Iz zapisok po teorii slovesnosti* (Kharkov, 1905), p.
263.

relation and exteriority on the other, it would not be difficult to recognize metaphor and metonymy.

Specific Taxonomies

Most of the time, however, observers are seeking to describe the relations within symbolism in an autonomous fashion, and do not compare the results of this effort with those produced by the semantic study of discourse. (The separation is clearly regrettable, all the more so in that only such a comparison would allow us to pose this pertinent question: since tropes can be made explicit in propositions, and implications can be made explicit in inferences, why cannot any proposition at all be condensed into a trope, and any inference at all into an implication?) Two major classifications have dominated the Western tradition; they both go back to Aristotle, but to different texts. Moreover, first impressions notwithstanding, they are not completely independent of each other.

The first has its origin in the *Poetics,* where Aristotle evokes four classes of transpositions (the term "metaphor" has a generic meaning in this instance): "either from genus to species, or from species to genus, or from species to species, or on grounds of analogy" (1457b). Leaving aside for the moment the analogical relation, which is visibly opposed to the other three taken as a whole, we note that we are dealing here with a combinatorial having two dimensions, species-genus and input-output (or direct meaning and indirect meaning), of which three products are listed whereas the fourth is lacking: from genus to genus. These products could be designated by the prevailing rhetorical terms: from genus to species = particularizing synecdoche; from species to genus = generalizing synecdoche; from species to species = metaphor. The missing type, from genus to genus, corresponds to metonymy: whereas metaphor implies two terms (species) having a common property (genus)—for example, "love" and "flame" are both "burning"—metonymy requires that one term (species) be describable in terms of two independent properties, or decomposable into (at least) two contiguous parts—for example, as Catholic doctrine and its geographic seat are two aspects of one entity, the former can be designated by the name of the latter: "Rome." If, as Potebnia maintained, metaphor implies a common predicate for two different subjects, metonymy in contrast requires that a given subject be endowed with two different predicates.

Curiously enough, this very "logical" classification has enjoyed little popularity. We find an echo of it in the eighteenth century, in Lessing: in his treatises on fables he contrasts *allegory*, designation of one particular by another particular, and *example*, designation of the general by a particular. The terms "general" and "particular" are indeed convertible into "genus" and "species," but it is also true that example and allegory designate varieties of propositional, not lexical, symbolism (I shall return to this point). We can also refer to Schelling's *Philosophy of Art*, where allegory is defined as the passage from the particular to the general, and schematism as the passage from the general to the particular (whereas the "symbol" is the interpenetration of the two). But that is about as far as we can go.

Another Aristotelian classification has met with a better fate. Aristotle did not apply it to tropes, but to associations in general: in the second chapter of his treatise on memory, he stated that associations may be based upon resemblance, proximity, and opposition. Augustine later transposed this categorization to tropes (and to etymological relations) in one of his early works, *On Dialectics*, and from that point on it is found throughout the history of Western rhetoric (in this area Cicero and Quintilian are content to enumerate; they do not classify). It is no doubt the more concrete and evocative, more "psychological" character of these labels that has assured them such success. The list has undergone minor modifications, moreover. In Gerardus Joannes Vossius we find four basic relations: participation has a place alongside the others. In Beauzée we find only three, but not quite the same ones: opposition is missing. In Roman Jakobson, of course, we go back to just two, resemblance and contiguity; but Kenneth Burke can still speak of "four master tropes," metaphor, metonymy, synecdoche, and irony, a list which matches that of Vossius. It is in this context that we can most easily understand why metaphor, a trope of resemblance, has enjoyed the greatest popularity of all the tropes: it is because resemblance, unlike contiguity and the rest, reproduces the relation that underlies any symbolic evocation, that is, a certain form of equation, of "superposition," since a first meaning makes it possible to evoke a second one. Metaphor is thus, as it were, the clearest incarnation of the symbolic relation: it is equivalence (resemblance) to the second power, whereas metonymy combines heterogeneous elements: equivalence and contiguity. At the same time, evocations through resemblance have a cumulative effect (all parts of a text may symbolize the same thing), whereas evocations through contiguity or coexistence are distributive (a particular association corresponds to each segment of the text).

The difficulty with this classification arises from its arbitrary character. Why should there be only three types of association, or four, or two? It is in order to correct this arbitrariness that Jakobson has attempted to link the two types of association with two basic linguistic processes, selection and combination (categories which we have seen operating in the rhetorical tradition, particularly in Cicero). But the most successful attempt to make explicit the bases for this classification remains so far as I am concerned that of the Dubois *Rhétorique générale,* which has in its favor the fact that it brings Aristotle's two classifications together: participation is equivalent to inclusion (passage from genus to species or from

74

species to genus); resemblance is equivalent to the passage from one species to another; contiguity, to the passage from one genus to another through the intermediary of a common species.

The same categorization can be transposed to the level of propositions: Aristotle and Lessing had begun to do this. We speak of *example* or *illustration* when a particular proposition evokes a general truth, of *aphorism* in the opposite case (this is Schelling's *schematism*). The term *allegory* could be defined here as a "symbolic relation of resemblance between propositions" (Christian *typology* would be a variant of this), whereas we reserve the term *implication* for contiguity or coexistence; *allusion* would be equally suitable in certain cases. The chart below sums up these terminological propositions.

"LOGICAL" TERMINOLOGY	"PSYCHOLOGICAL" TERMINOLOGY	LEXICAL SYMBOLISM	PROPOSITIONAL SYMBOLISM
particular-general species-genus	participation, generalization	generalizing synecdoche	example, illustration
general-particular, genus-species	participation, particularization	particularizing synecdoche	aphorism, schematism
particular-particular, species-species	resemblance, comparison	metaphor	allegory, typology
general-general, genus-genus	contiguity, coexistence	metonymy	implication, allusion

This initial grid may of course be complicated *ad infinitum* by further subdivisions. Let us note for future reference the difference already indicated by Aristotle between simple metaphor and analogical metaphor (or, in Peirce's terms, between image and diagram, two varieties of icon); or the difference Quintilian recognized between material synecdoche (part-whole) and conceptual synecdoche (genus-species); or the one that makes it possible to separate two types of synecdoche, particularization and generalization on the one hand, personification and autonomasia on the other (which is simply the difference between common noun and proper noun). Many others can be found in ancient and modern rhetorical treatises.

When a concrete evocation occurs, several operations come into play in sequence, although we perceive them simultaneously. When Mr. Longdon draws the conclusion that we have noted regarding Mr. Vanderbank's character, he proceeds by generalization (Vanderbank's statement is an example of the betrayal of friends), then by implication (to betray one's friends is to manifest a vulgar mind), and he ends up with a new particularization (Vanderbank is a creature who shares in this vulgarity of mind)—which he never expresses, moreover, in this direct form; he contents himself with saying, in effect: I find you very different from people of my generation.

I have attempted to summarize here the taxonomic efforts of the rhetoricians of the past; and yet the importance—the popularity, even—that the debates over these terms have assumed seems to me largely undeserved. The interest of a classification like this one is purely practical; as it is, it includes no hypothesis as to the nature of symbolic phenomena. Once we have granted ourselves two terms, general and particular, we can categorize all the objects in the world into the classes that result from their combination; it is certainly more convenient to handle sets that are smaller than the set of all symbolic phenomena, but this says nothing about the nature of the objects being classified. It might be possible, however, to discover a psychological counterpart to these categories (as Jakobson has suggested for resemblance and contiguity), in which case the subdivisions would become pertinent once again.

The Paronymic Detour

The associations of which I have just been speaking all make connections among fragments of the world (objects, actions, and the like); it is no accident that only morphemes with referential value can serve as input for symbolic associations (unlike conjunctions, prepositions, and so on). This must not lead us to believe that associative relations between words are impossible; the intertextual relations evoked earlier are an example to the contrary. Even in an association based on the signified, the signifiers can play a role; but then the characteristic feature of this latter relation is its inability to exist without the other: even if it has not been sought, semantic motivation necessarily reinforces phonic or graphic resemblance. Thus we shall speak, in such cases, of a *paronymic detour* (paronyms are words that are similar in form but independent in meaning), optional and therefore secondary with respect to the semantic relation, but capable of greatly magnifying its intensity: the speaker associates language with his own point of view, as it were, since this point of view apparently goes along with that of words. The composition of the lexicon, unchallengeable and honorable object that it is, confirms his utterance (just as, conversely, we have only to juxtapose two things in order to notice their similarity, as we have seen). The paronymic detour follows the same paths in symbolic evocation as in discursive predication (where it is easier to observe). The three historically constituted areas in which its role seems most important are etymological reasoning, poetry, and word play.

Etymological reasoning seeks to prove kinship of meaning by proximity of form; it transcends etymological research proper, as practiced in our time, that sort of etymological research which is interested only in the historical affiliation of forms: in Plato (the *Cratylus*), formal and semantic affinity does not pass for historical; in Heidegger, the original meaning is also the true meaning. Etymological reasoning (which Jean Paulhan called "proof by etymology") is also produced spontaneously, independently of grammar and philosophy: in this case we speak of popular etymology, an easy source of deliberate humor (Estienne Tabourot des Accords: parliament

[Fr. *parlement*] is a place where people speak [*on parle*] and tell lies [*on ment*]) or involuntary humor (J.-P. Brisset's version of the descent of man from frogs).

It seems at first glance that it is a long way from popular etymology to poetry. But when the poet rhymes *songe* ["dream"] with *mensonge* ["lie"], what is he doing but establishing a harmonious and satisfying relation, although a temporary one, between form and meaning: satisfying because it fulfills that obscure aspiration to order which is at the very root of popular etymology. . . . To be a poet, according to Mallarmé, is to "give a purer meaning to the words of the tribe." There would then be something like an unconscious poetry in giving a word a meaning apparently more appropriate to its phonetic structure: this would be the case of a word like *fruste* ["worn," "corroded," "rough," "unpolished"] juxtaposed through its meaning with *brusque* ["blunt," "abrupt," "brusque," "rough," "uncivil"] and *rustre* ["boorish," "clownish," "rude"].[2]

The paronymic principle, itself a variant of the law of parallelism, is perhaps not as important for poetry as people have a tendency to proclaim every hundred years or so, as they discover anew the power of sounds. Still, it is no less a part of the very definition of poetic discourse.

When Humpty Dumpty explains that *slithy* signifies *lithe* and *slimy*, or that *mimsy* signifies *flimsy* and *miserable*, he finds, as if by accident, synonyms that are also paronyms: the semantic relationship is made explicit, but the language agrees with Humpty Dumpty. When Ludwig Hevesi says of an Italian poet who is antimilitaristic at heart but who is obliged to celebrate the German emperor in verse: "Being unable to drive out the Caesars, he at least managed to wipe out the caesuras," he seems to be juxtaposing nothing but similar sounds; but "Caesar" and "caesura," terms that are unrelated in the lexicon, become antonyms in this discursive

---

[2]John Orr, *Essais d'étymologie et de philologie françaises* (Paris, 1963), p. 7.

context, where what is essential is opposed to what is insignificant. In these word plays, as in all puns, whether in "good" or "bad" taste, the relation of meaning is grounded in or justified by that of sounds.

But the latter never replaces or excludes the former.

Indeterminacy of Meaning?

Indeterminacy of the Symbolic

One obvious and radical difference between entailment in discourse and symbolic evocation lies in the fact that the one is objectively present whereas the other is produced only in the consciousness of speaker and hearer. Because of this, the latter can never have the same degree of specificity and certainty as the former; it can only come more or less close. Try as we may to achieve maximum determination for it, symbolic evocation can never equal the explicitness of discourse.

Even if the indirect meaning is apparently present, as is the case for example with metaphors of the *in praesentia* type, the very fact of bringing together the two meanings, of establishing an equivalence between them, can be interpreted in countless ways. The most explicit comparison, the one that spells out the motive for linking the two terms, nevertheless always opens up the possibility of seeking out another association. Comparison is inherently double, with an antecedent (discursive) equivalence and a consequent (symbolic) equivalence, to use Paul Henle's terms. Writers have always understood this: even when their comparisons are openly motivated, they are set up to generate associations on other levels. Describing the child who will grow up to be Saint Julian, Flaubert writes: "With his pink cheeks and blue eyes, he looked like a little Jesus." The comparison is motivated by physical resemblance (this is the antecedent part) but it also gives rise to the idea of future sainthood (the consequent part): we had a similar example in "immaculate as the floor of a church." During the scene of the slaughter of the animals, "the sky appeared like a sheet of blood": the color is obviously only the springboard for other associations, and blood is present here through many of its properties in addition to color.

Recognizing the indeterminacy that constitutes any *in absentia* evocation is one thing; seeing every symbolic process as essentially indeterminate or—what amounts to more or less the same thing—placing all symbolic phenomena on a scale of values whose highest position would be occupied by the least determined symbol is clearly something else again. And yet since the romantic era, through all the "symbolist" and "surrealist" vicissitudes, the efforts of Western theoreticians and poets have tended toward making the indeterminate a positive value. The romantics did postulate that the symbolic field had two opposite poles, calling them "allegory" and "symbol," but their preference for the latter is so obvious that allegories appear only as failed symbols. Now it is indeed the inexhaustible and thus untranslatable character of the one form that opposes it to the other, which is closed and determined by nature—whatever terms are chosen to designate them. In the symbol, Humboldt said, the idea "remains forever out of reach in itself"; "Even stated in every language," Goethe added, "it remains unsayable." The same is true of the opposition between comparison and symbol, for Hegel, or between prose and poetry, for A. W. Schlegel: "The nonpoetic view of things is the one that sees them as controlled by sense perceptions and by the determinations of reason; the poetic view is the one that interprets them continuously and finds in them an inexhaustible figurative character."

Degrees of Indeterminacy

A more balanced view of the situation would consist in supposing that there is a (quantitative) difference between strongly and weakly determined evocations, while abstaining, at the outset, from making any value judgment. This opposition between symbolic expressions whose new meaning can be established and those in which such a specification is impossible seems to have been first examined in a detailed and unbiased way by ʿAbd al-Qāhir al-Jurjānī, in the eleventh century. According to Jurjânî, tropes are of two kinds: they have to do either with the intellect or with the imagination. Tropes of intellect are those whose meaning is established immediately and unequivocally; the statement conveyed may consequently be true or false, for example, when one says "I have seen a lion" in speaking of a man (Greek, Sanskrit, and Arab rhetorics coincide curiously in the choice of this example: Achilles, Devadata and Ahmed are all "lions"). Tropes of imagination, on the other hand, point to no particular object; thus what they state is neither true nor false; the search for their meanings is a prolonged process, if not an endless one. They are "impossible to limit except by approximation," and the poet who uses them "is like a person who is dipping into an inexhaustible pool of water, or the one who is extracting an inexhaustible mineral." What object, Jurjānī asks, is indicated by the expression "the reins of morning," or "the hands of the wind," or "the horses of youth"? It is not easy to decide (*Asrār al-balāgha, The Mysteries of Eloquence*). In the modern period, Philip Wheelwright makes a comparable effort in his *Metaphor and Reality;* he opposes the indeterminate *diaphor* to the *epiphor,* in which associations are more strictly controlled.

Romantic and postromantic writing (like earlier writing) attempted to cultivate "diaphor" to the detriment of "epiphor," thus earning a reputation for obscurity. Obscurity itself is not a uniform, unanalysable phenomenon; its causes vary. A few examples may help to illustrate their diversity and make us more familiar with the problematics of indeterminacy.

Nerval's *Chimeras,* especially "El Desdichado" and "Artemis," looked to readers of Nerval's day, as they do to us, like hermeneutic texts. However, their obscurity is of a special sort. Let us examine the last six lines of "El Desdichado."

> Am I Amor or Phoebus?... Lusignan or Biron?
> My forehead is still red with the kiss of the queen;
> In the grotto where the siren swims I have had a dream...
>
> And twice I have crossed and conquered the Acheron:
> On Orpheus' lyre in turn I have sent
> The cries of faery and the signs of a saint.[1]

Confronted with these lines, even the critic most dedicated to the "immanent" or "structural" method finds himself obliged to take recourse to historical research. The abundance of proper names is revealing: before we can ask why Nerval has brought these characters together as he has, we must become aware of the set of historical associations attached to their names: Amor, Phoebus, Lusignan, Biron, Acheron, Orpheus. Even if this approach does not automatically dissipate the text's obscurity, it begins to weaken it: an exploration of collective memory is thus indispensable. Similarly, though the four female characters are not given proper names, they send us back nevertheless to other texts which, once called to mind, allow us to overcome the difficulty (for example, we have to be familiar with the episode of the fairy Melusine's cries when she is separated from Lusignan). If the poem is obscure, it is because a specific body of knowledge exists which the reader lacks; once this knowledge is supplied, the path to understanding is open (of course, this is

---

[1] *Selected Writings of Gérard de Nerval,* trans. Geoffrey Wagner (Florence, 1957), p. 213.

only a beginning). "The fairy" or "Amor" are not indeterminate terms left for the reader to interpret as he pleases, not invitations to free-associate, but, quite to the contrary, terms whose evocations are strictly controlled. Truth exists; but the path leading to it is hard to follow.

The obscurity of a Rimbaud is of a different sort entirely.

To be more precise, in the *Illuminations* (we shall consider only this one text), we find difficulties of two orders. The first ones, comparable after all to those we found in Nerval, stem from problems involving the *referent*. The sentences that make up the text are comprehensible in themselves, but the object that they evoke is never named, and thus we may hesitate as to its identification (*H* is the clearest example from this series); or else, once named, it fails to fit our ordinary representations of the given type of objects (for example, *Promontory*); or again, the object designated is charged with symbolic associations that we do not manage to specify (*Royalty*). What all these cases, despite their differences, have in common is that their difficulty is referential in nature, and not properly semantic: we have no trouble understanding the sentences, but we hesitate as to the identity of their referent (whose existence is nevertheless not in doubt) or the associations attached to this referent.

Another type of difficulty arises in the *Illuminations*, however, a type at least as abundantly represented as the former; here the obscurity has entirely different sources. In his treatise on hermeneutics, *On Christian Doctrine*, Augustine recognized two types of difficulties for interpretation (and thus, implicitly, two forms of symbolism): those that have to do with the comprehension of discourse, and those that depend on our knowledge of things (II, xvi, 23). Similarly, in Rimbaud, after the difficulties that are independent of discourse, we stumble over those that are due entirely to *discourse itself*. The intelligibility of discourse demands a certain degree of coherence that Rimbaud's texts do not always offer.

If we do not wish to give up the possibility of understanding them, we are obliged to follow the path of symbolic evocation. But this path proves to be different here from what it may have been elsewhere.

The most frequently manifested incoherence in the *Illuminations* arises between sentences. In these texts Rimbaud writes as if he were unaware of anaphor: two sentences, even though adjacent, do not refer to each other, nor to the same referent. A passage from *Childhood* (iii) illustrates this device in an almost caricatural way:

> In the woods there is a bird; his song stops you and makes you blush.
> There is a clock that never strikes.
> There is a hollow with a nest of white beasts.
> There is a cathedral that goes down and a lake that goes up.[2]

Here the objects, all situated on the same level, are perfectly heterogeneous, and yet they are unified: referentially, by the common circumstance of being "in the woods," and linguistically, by the parallelism of the constructions, which all begin by "there is."

In *After the Deluge* we must be satisfied with the idea that the place where all the events occur in proximity to one another is simply the universe, and that the time is "after the deluge":

> In the dirty main street, stalls were set up and boats were hauled toward the sea, high tiered as in old prints.
> Blood flowed at Blue Beard's,—through slaughterhouses, in circuses, where the windows were blanched by God's seal.
> Blood and milk flowed.
> Beavers built. "Mazagrans" smoked in the little bars.
> In the big glass house, still dripping, children in mourning looked at the marvelous pictures. [P. 3]

2 *Illuminations and Other Prose Poems*, trans. Louise Varèse (New York, 1957), p. 11.

The difficulty in understanding such a text stems not only from the dearth of information available on each of the objects evoked (stalls, boats, windows, blood, milk, beavers, bars, house, children, pictures...), even though in the French original each one is introduced by the definite article, as if its identification were self-evident. We are at least as much hindered by the dearth of relations among the given objects—and thus by the absence of what makes these sentences a *single* discourse.

The difficulty increases as we descend to lower units of language. Here is the third section of *Youth:*

> Instructive voices exiled... Physical candor bitterly quelled...—Adagio.—Ah! the infinite egotism of adolescence, the studious optimism: how the world was full of flowers that summer! Airs and forms dying...—A choir to calm impotence and absence! A choir of glasses, of nocturnal melodies... Quickly, indeed, the nerves take up the chase. [P. 145]

And a paragraph from *Anguish:*

> (O palms! diamond!—Love! strength!—higher than all joys and all fame!—in this case, everywhere—demon, god,—Youth of this being: myself!) [P. 95]

Unlike Nerval's text, this one has no proper names, whose referent or customary associations we might fail to know; the words used belong to everyday vocabulary. What are lacking are explicit discursive associations: we do not know what relations unite these words, these phrases (mere succession is not enough), just as, in the preceding examples, we did not know what justified the presence and the order of the sentences, which were all nevertheless adequately clear in themselves. The associations made explicit in discourse are the base on which the implicit associations of each reader are strung together; the interpretive process is radically changed when the symbolic evocations, however ingenious they may be, find themselves deprived of a pedestal: they more or less float in the air. The result is not, as one might have imagined, a situation in which it is impossible to supplement the discursive relations with symbolic relations, but rather, on the contrary, an overabundance of symbolic associations, among which the absence of discursive underpinnings makes it impossible to choose. There are not too few but too many ways to bring together these unfinished sentences of *Youth* into a whole.

Discontinuity and incoherence are not the only reasons why the Rimbaldian discourse is obscure in itself. Another lies in the difficulty we have in identifying the referent of each expression taken separately. One always has the feeling that Rimbaud names the closest genus instead of calling the object by its own name; hence the impression of great abstraction that these texts leave; we never succeed in descending from genus to species. What is "repose in the light" (*Vigils* I)? "a black powder [that] rains on my vigil" and "violet frondescence [that] falls" (*Phrases*)? What is "the consuming work that is gathering and growing in the masses" (*Youth* I), or the "magnetic comedy" (*Side Show*)? Here the referent is not simply hidden; it is by its very essence inaccessible. The result of the various semantic transformations that we see at work in Rimbaud is impressive, and new: we are confronted with a text that is structurally (and no longer simply by virtue of historical contingencies) *undecidable,* rather like those equations with several unknowns that can have an indefinite number of solutions.

What is the meaning of a sequence like "fires in the rain of the wind of diamonds... " (*Barbarian*)? One commentator has suggested that this be taken as a typographical error, the words "of the wind" having strayed from the line above. What strikes me as remarkable in this case is the very possibility of hesitation between a printing error and an intentional formulation: the very nature of Rimbaud's text is precisely what makes made hesitation possible, what has conquered a legitimate place within literature for such undecidable texts. The historical importance of this gesture, in the light of what has happened to Western poetry in recent years, seems to me hard to overestimate.

The requirement that the text be read "literally and in all senses" (which also means "in no sense") has become the distinguishing feature of modern poetry, and subsequently of criticism. But behind one and the same demand for indeterminacy of meaning, different realities are often hidden and revealed.

Symbolist poetry had a similar requirement in its program. First, the poet was to symbolize rather than to signify. As Mallarmé said, "to name an object is to suppress three-quarters of the pleasure of the poem, which derives from the satisfaction of guessing little by little; to suggest the object is the dream." Or again: "I believe that there must be only allusion." And as Anatole France exclaimed indignantly: "Express no longer, only suggest. This is the heart of the entire new poetics." Furthermore, symbolization was not to have a precise object: this is exactly where the symbol is superior to allegory. Maeterlinck, for example, appropriating the well-known romantic distinction, illustrated the symbolist ideal. We have already seen the degree to which the "indices" calling for interpretation were numerous and insistent in his case: repetitions within lines or between scenes; narrative irrelevancy of remarks or sequences, and thus discontinuity; unwarranted attention paid to insignificant details—which leads the reader to conclude that, in order to be justified, these details must have meaning elsewhere. But in fact that meaning is never spelled out. For example, Pelleas and Melisande, at the seaside, exchange the following remarks:

Melisande: Something is leaving the port...
Pelleas: It must be a big ship... (. . .)

Melisande: The ship is in the light...It is already very far away...
Pelleas: It flies away under full sail... (. . .)
Melisande: Why does it go away tonight?... One can hardly see it any longer... Perhaps it will be wrecked...
Pelleas: The night falls very quickly... (. . .)
Pelleas: Nothing can be seen any longer on the sea...
Melisande: I see more lights.[3]

This exchange of information about the boat, the sea, and the lights has no narrative justification; but precisely for this reason the spectator judges that there is another, "symbolic" justification. Having reached this point, unless he refers to preestablished external codes, he gets no precise determination from the work. We may wonder whether the great success of these plays in their day, and their equally impressive obscurity today, is not connected with this very property of symbolist writing: it implies complicity on the part of the reader-listener, who at every moment has to supply the missing meanings, to profit from the fact that the words have been set to resonating. This the reader of a different era, no longer communicating in the same atmosphere, cannot do—and the text falls on its face, for it is no longer supported by the kind of reception that it solicits. With Maeterlinck as with Rimbaud there is indeterminacy of meaning; but the difference is enormous. The one produces a revolution in language, the other asks his readers to daydream over insignificant sentences.

In our day, the narratives of Franz Kafka have come to constitute another characteristic example of indeterminacy of meaning. The strangeness of these texts is known to have driven their first interpreters to consider them as "thinly disguised parables" of something else—but in fact agreement has never been reached on the nature of that other thing. Is it an essentially religious problematics? Or an anticipation of the unhappiness of a far too materialistic and bureaucratic

[3]Trans. Richard Hovey (New York, 1915), pp. 32–34.

89

world? Or else Kafka's own struggles, his relationship with his father, his difficulty in marrying? The very abundance of interpretations renders them suspect, and it has led a second wave of exegetes to proclaim that the distinctive feature of Kafka's texts is that they lend themselves to a multiplicity of interpretations without authenticating any one of them. As Wilhelm Emrich wrote:

> *All* possible interpretations are kept open; each one maintains a certain plausibility; none is unequivocally certain. . . . Characteristic of Kafka's writing, however, is the very fact that it is no longer possible to establish any unequivocally determinable meaning "behind" the phenomena, proceedings, and utterances.[4]

If we suppose that this is indeed the case, by what means does Kafka produce this effect of undecidable symbolism? Marthe Robert has proposed the following explanation: the events themselves that are represented in his narratives are never anything but instances of interpretation—and of impossible interpretation; the symbolic is at once the constructive principle and the fundamental theme of the text.

> All of Kafka's narratives contain with the same clarity the pattern of that desperate struggle on the part of the hero to know what to make of the truth of symbols.[5]

> [Consequently,] Kafka's hero is in exactly the same situation as his exegete . . .; he too has to deal with symbols, he too believes spontaneously in them, hastily finds for them a meaning according to which he believes he can govern his life, but precisely in that he is perpetually fooled.[6]

[4] *Franz Kafka: A Critical Study of His Writings,* trans. S. Z. Buehne (New York, 1968), pp. 82–83.
[5] *Kafka* (Paris, 1960), p. 120.
[6] *Sur le papier* (Paris, 1967), pp. 191–192.

Joseph K. tries in vain to know why justice is pursuing him, K. the surveyor is embarked upon a desperate quest for the identity of the castle, and the condemned man of the *Penal Colony* does not succeed in deciphering his sentence until the moment when, penetrating deeply into his body, it kills him. There is thus an irreducible opposition, as it were, and one which is profoundly disturbing for interpretation, between the clarity of the allegorical apparatus Kafka has set up and the obscurity of the message he is delivering, between the textual invitation to allegorize everything and the narrative impossibility of finding the meaning—the latter becoming the message of the former.

These examples certainly do not exhaust the forms of "obscurity" in modern literature, the variety that indeterminacy of meaning manifests there. But they illustrate, on the one hand, the very existence of this variety (or, if one prefers, the imprecision of terms such as "obscure," "indeterminate," "polyvalent," and so on), and, on the other hand, the necessary presence of quite special conditions for separating the "undecidable" texts from the others. A separation that introduces a difference and opens the way to a lucid analysis, rather than locking us into the sterile mystique of the ineffable.

PART II /

STRATEGIES OF INTERPRETATION

The art of interpretation can reveal
itself fully only in *semiotic* works.
—Friedrich Schlegel

I have already made clear my position on the difference between describing the *general* conditions in which symbolic as well as interpretive activities occur, and studying the *particular* choices made from among all the possible ones by a given literary genre or a given exegetic strategy: a difference in level, which leads at the same time to two complementary perspectives, theoretical and historical. The second part of this book will thus allow me to go into detail concerning some of the categories set forth up to now, and to put them to the test: to what extent does theory enable us to account for historical reality?

In order to carry out this task, I have chosen, first, to concentrate on interpretation (as opposed to production), since the interpretive side seemed to me to have been less thoroughly explored. Next, I have singled out two major exegetic schools from among many others—both because their influence has been stronger than any other, and because their historical articulation appears to me to be a rich source of instruction. These two are patristic and philological exegeses. My study of these strategies does not pretend to originality on the historical level; rather, it aims to add a necessary complement to the general presentation that has preceded.

A Finalist Interpretation:
Patristic Exegesis

Triggers for Interpretation

The first example is that of a strategy that has remained dominant in the Western world longer than any other: biblical exegesis, as it developed in the early centuries of Christianity and was perpetuated up to about the seventeenth century. I have chosen the writings of Saint Augustine as my basic text, but I will add occasional references to those who prepared the way for him or to those—far more numerous—who followed.[1]

[1]The question of Augustinian exegesis has been abundantly treated in the scholarly literature. Here are a number of useful references: E. Moirat, *Notion augustinienne de l'herméneutique* (Clermont-Ferrand, 1906); Marie Comeau, *Saint Augustin, exégète du 4ᵉ Évangile* (Paris, 1930); Henri Irénée Marrou, *Saint Augustin et la fin de la culture antique* (Paris, 1938); Maurice Pontet, *L'exégèse de Saint Augustin prédicateur* (Paris, 1945); Jean Pépin, "Saint Augustin et la fonction protreptique de l'allégorie," *Recherches augustiniennes* (Paris, 1958), pp. 243–286; Jean Pépin, "A propos de l'histoire de l'exégèse allégorique, l'absurdité signe de l'allégorie," in *Studia patristica*, vol. i, Berlin, 1957, pp. 395–413; Gerhard Strauss, *Schriftgebrauch, Schriftauslegung und Schriftbeweis bei Augustin* (Tübingen, 1959); Ulrich Duchrow, *Sprachverständnis und biblisches Hören bei Augustinus* (Tübingen, 1965). See also the relevant sections of histories of hermeneutics such as Ceslaus Spicq, *Esquisse d'une histoire de l'exégèse latine au Moyen Age* (Paris, 1944); Jean Pépin, *Mythe et allégorie*, (Paris, 1958: 2d ed., 1977); Henri de Lubac, *Exégèse médiévale, Les quatre sens de l'Ecriture*, 4 vols. (Paris, 1959–64); Robert M. Grant, *A Short History of the Interpretation of the Bible* (New York, 1963). Augustine's crucial treatise, *On Christian Doctrine* (abbreviated OCD) is quoted in the D. W. Robertson translation (Indianapolis, 1958).

General Principle

Interpretation (as opposed to comprehension) is not an automatic process, as we have seen; something within the text or outside it has to indicate that the immediately accessible meaning is insufficient, must be taken only as the starting point of an inquiry whose end result will be a second meaning. What index triggers exegesis here?

The patristic strategy includes a detailed response to this question. But in effect all its details add up to a single principle, which is the following. At the outset, there is not just one meaning, there are already two: the immediate meaning of the words that make up the biblical text, and the meaning that we know the Bible has because it is, as Saint Paul said, divinely inspired. For simplicity's sake we shall call this latter meaning Christian doctrine. Interpretation is born of the gap (which is not a necessary one, but which frequently exists) between these two meanings; it is nothing other than the course which allows us to relate, and thus to identify, the one with the other, by means of a series of equivalences.

The index that triggers interpretation is thus not found in the text itself but in its ceaseless confrontation with another text (that of Christian doctrine) and in the possible difference between the two. Augustine could hardly be clearer on this point: interpretation has to be practiced on each and every figurative expression. Now how are we to discover that an expression is not to be taken in its literal meaning?

> A method of determining whether a locution is literal or figurative must be established. And generally this method consists in this: that whatever appears in the divine Word that does not literally pertain to virtuous behavior or to the truth of faith, you must take to be figurative. [*OCD*, III, x, 14]

This principle is so all-inclusive and general that the task of triggering is not necessarily regulated in any explicit way:

it always suffices to refer to the principle. It nevertheless remains possible to list more special cases in which the principle is adapted to concrete circumstances; in such cases, properties inherent in the text itself signal the necessity for interpretation.

Doctrinal Implausibilities

In the first place, all passages that openly contradict Christian doctrine are figurative and thus must be interpreted. Consequently, we are dealing with an *in absentia* contradiction, with a doctrinal implausibility. Here is the rule as Augustine formulated it:

> If a locution is admonitory, condemning either vice or crime or commending either utility or beneficence, it is not figurative. But if it seems to commend either vice or crime or to condemn either utility or beneficence, it is figurative. [*OCD*, III, xvi, 24].

> Those things which seem almost shameful to the inexperienced, whether simply spoken or actually performed either by the person of God or by men whose sanctity is commended to us, are all figurative, and their secrets are to be removed as kernels from the husk as nourishment for charity. [The example follows:] Thus no reasonable person would believe under any circumstances that the feet of the Lord were anointed with precious ointment by the woman in the manner of lecherous and dissolute men whose banquets we despise. For the good odor is good fame which anyone in the works of a good life will have when he follows in the footsteps of Christ, as if anointing His feet with a most precious odor. In this way what is frequently shameful in other persons is in a divine or prophetic person the sign of some great truth. [*OCD*, III, xii, 18]

Material Implausibilities

In the second place, the biblical text does not even have to offend against the Christian religion; it is enough for it to contradict ordinary good sense, common knowledge. This is no longer a doctrinal but a material implausibility, as it were. Augustine is just as explicit on this point: "When the sense is absurd if it is taken verbally, it is to be inquired whether or not what is said is expressed in this or that trope which we do not know" (*OCD*, III, xxix, 41). Here is the way this rule is applied:

> An index must indeed warn the reader that this narrative is not to be understood in the carnal sense: for green plants and fruit trees constitute the nourishment that *Genesis* attributes to all species of animals, to all birds as to all serpents; now we see clearly that lions feed exclusively on meat.... Why does the Holy Spirit introduce certain statements which seem absurd when applied to the visible world, if not to force us, since we are unable to understand them in the literal sense, to seek their spiritual meanings? [*In. Ps.*, 77, 26–27]

Superfluities

In the third place, finally, it is not necessary that the biblical text besmirch God or his faithful ones, or even that it offend against reason; it may simply contain fragments whose usefulness for Christian doctrine is not evident. This produces the figure of superfluity, an index that consists in the absence of the positive rather than the presence of the negative. Augustine discusses this in another text: we are to consider as figurative not only what, taken literally, would be shocking, but also what would be useless from the religious point of view (*De Gen. ad. litt.*, IX, 12, 22).

A certain similarity among these various devices is apparent: in no case do we discover the existence of a second meaning, and thus the necessity for interpretation, by confronting segments that are copresent in the text; the implausibilities and superfluities that Augustine codified all result from the recollection of another text, present only in memory, which is

Christian doctrine itself. In other words, the indices that trigger interpretation in patristic strategy are paradigmatic, not syntagmatic. This is also what differentiates one strategy from another; if I had taken the rabbinical gloss as my example, we would have found the opposite distribution. But, naturally, what is still more characteristic of patristic exegesis is the absence of the need for formal indices to determine whether a text is to be interpreted or not; the obligation to interpret is given, as it were, in advance.

The Choice of Interpretable Segments

In patristic exegesis, any segment at all of the text may become the object of interpretation, provided that it falls under the auspices of the general principle. Nevertheless, some segments by their very nature do call for interpretation more often than others. The patristic strategy does not seem particularly original in this respect, for we find a similar tendency to be selective in other contemporary interpretive strategies.

The principle that appears to underlie the reasons for choosing one segment as opposed to another is the following: the *poorer* the *linguistic meaning,* and thus the more limited its comprehension, the more easily *symbolic evocation* is grafted onto it, and thus the *richer* the interpretation. As the lexicon does contain words that are particularly limited in meaning, those are the ones that will be chosen in preference to others as material for interpretation.

Proper nouns

The word class that is poorest in meanings is obviously that of proper nouns. Which explains why they receive particular attention in almost every exegetic tradition. Augustine is only following custom here:

> Many Hebrew names which are not explained by the authors of those books undoubtedly have considerable importance in clarifying the enigmas of the Scriptures, if someone were able to interpret them. Some men, expert in that language, have rendered no small benefit to posterity by having explained all of those words taken from the Scriptures without reference to place and have translated Adam, Eve, Abraham, Moses, and names of places like Jerusalem, Sion, Jericho, Sinai, Lebanon, Jordan, or whatever other names in that language are unknown to us. [*OCD*, II, xvi, 23]

Proper nouns, and preferably foreign ones (that are thus still less comprehensible). Augustine finds a purely Christian justification in this practice: did Christ not prove, by giving a new name to Simon (Peter), that names are not arbitrary?

Numbers

Although they are indeed poorest in meanings, proper nouns are not alone in satisfying the exegetic requirement. Another example of very frequently interpreted linguistic segments is provided by numbers (which are not "asemic" but "monosemic"). Augustine again bears witness to this:

> An ignorance of numbers also causes many things expressed figuratively and mystically in the Scriptures to be misunderstood. Certainly, a gifted and frank person cannot avoid wondering about the significance of the fact that Moses, Elias, and the Lord Himself all fasted for forty days. The knot, as it were, of this figurative action cannot be untied without a knowledge and consideration of this number. For it contains four tens, to indicate the knowledge of all things involved in times. The day and the year both run their courses in a quaternion.... Again, the number ten signifies a knowledge of the Creator and the creature; for the trinity is the Creator and the

septenary indicates the creature by reason of his life and body. For with reference to life there are three, whence we should love God with all our hearts, with all our souls, and with all our minds; and with reference to the body there are very obviously four elements of which it is made. Thus when the number ten is suggested to us with reference to time, or, that is, when it is multiplied by four, we are admonished to live chastely and continently without temporal delight, or, that is, to fast for forty days. This the Law, represented in the person of Moses; the Prophets, whose person is acted by Elias; and the Lord Himself all admonish. [*OCD*, II, xvi, 25]

Arithmological operations quickly attain a dizzying complexity, as we know. For large numbers must be reduced to small ones, the latter alone being endowed with a strictly determined meaning. The analysis to which Augustine subjects the number 153 (the number of fish caught in the miracle of the fishermen) is famous. First, $153 = 1 + 2 + \ldots + 17$; it is thus a "triangular" number. Now $17 = 10 + 7$, that is, the Law and the Holy Spirit. Or again, $153 = (50 \times 3) + 3$, but now 3 is the Trinity and $50 = (7 \times 7) + (1 \times 1)$, and so on (*Tract. in Joan.*, 122, 8, 1963). In neighboring traditions we could find still more complex examples that depend upon even more surprising associations.

Technical Nouns

Technical nouns are almost as poor in meanings as numbers. They are foreign to everyday vocabulary, and they designate, for example, a class of beings.

An ignorance of many . . . animals which are . . . used for comparison [in Scripture] is a great impediment to understanding. The same thing is true of stones, or of herbs or of other things that take root. For a knowledge of the carbuncle which shines in the darkness also illuminates many obscure places in books where it is used for similitudes, and an ignorance of beryl or of diamonds frequently closes the doors of understanding. In the same way it is not easy to grasp that the twig of olive which the dove brought when it returned to the ark signifies perpetual peace unless we know that the soft surface of oil is not readily corrupted by an alien liquid and that the olive tree is perennially in leaf. [OCD, ii, xvii, 24]

If a text speaks of carbuncles, or beryl, or of olive trees, it is doubtless not because of the things themselves but in view of the symbolic interpretation to which these species and thus these words are to be subjected.

We may suppose that each of these interpretations would have been much more difficult had it been applied to sentences made up of more common words, without proper nouns or numbers. But we are dealing here with a tendency of the language itself, and not with one imposed by a deliberate choice on the part of the fathers of the church.

Motivations; Concordances

Semantic Motivation

Both meanings, direct (that of the words of the Bible) and indirect (that of Christian doctrine), having been given in advance, interpretation will consist in showing that they are equivalent. Now the ways to establish semantic equivalence are not unlimited: this is done by following the paths of *lexical* symbolism (thus by abolishing the meaning of the initial statement in which the segment to be interpreted is embedded) or of *propositional* symbolism (by adding a second statement to the first). The choice is so limited that every interpretive practice necessarily falls back upon both possibilities. Thus, in the examples cited above, "good odor" is good reputation; the initial action has not really occurred, and thus we have a case of lexical symbolism. On the other hand,

Jesus did indeed stay forty days in the desert: the initial affirmation is maintained. But beyond this, the indication of the length of this sojourn implies something else: here we have an example of propositional symbolism. Associations might also be categorized as going from the general to the particular, from the particular to the general, from the particular to the particular, and so forth, forming figures such as the example, metaphor, synecdoche, and so on. We shall see a bit further on what particular form of motivation the patristic exegesis claims for itself; let us merely note here that it has a predilection for certain forms of propositional symbolism (the preservation of the literal meaning).

Paronymy

Semantic motivation is obligatory; it cannot be replaced, but it can be reinforced by motivation in the signifier, or paronymy. This latter in turn takes several forms: contamination (a single word is treated as an umbrella-word), notarikon (each letter of the word is interpreted as the initial letter of another word), ordinary puns, and so forth. All of these devices are found in patristic exegesis and specifically in Augustine, but they seem to come from the Judaic tradition.

Histories of exegesis neglect this sort of detail for the most part: the difference between syntagmatic and paradigmatic indices, the nature of interpretable segments, lexical or propositional motivation, the presence or absence of paronymyic detour. They are mistaken to do so, for the study of these choices can help shed light on specifically historical questions. One wonders, for example, whether Theagenes, "inventor" of the allegorical method, is not himself a later invention of the Stoic period, in which allegorical exegesis was widely practiced. But if the two exegetical practices look alike from a distance, they differ in their details: for example, among the Stoics, paronymic detour is almost obligatory;

with Theagenes, it never occurs. Or again, people have wondered whether Philo might not have borrowed his allegorical method from the Stoics. But the Stoics interpret proper nouns almost exclusively, whereas Philo spends more time on analyses of common nouns; he practices lexical symbolism and propositional symbolism simultaneously, whereas in this realm the Stoics limit themselves to the word alone. It would be easy to accumulate examples: one cannot overstress the mutual benefit that theory and history could derive in this area, if their encounters were more frequent.

Unity of Meaning

In establishing semantic equivalence, or motivation, one attributes to the word or to the sentence a meaning that it does not usually have. But such an interpretive strategy necessarily amounts to taking control of the semantic associations, and not to setting them free. Thus one must find *proofs* justifying this motivation, this relationship between two meanings, or better still, establishing that the two are in fact one and the same. This leads to a systematic search for other segments of the text in which the word—to which a new meaning is attributed here— already possesses this meaning, and uncontestably. Behind this search there lies a principle that is no less powerful for being unformulated: a word has, at bottom, only one meaning. This is what drives the exegete to seek harmony underneath the apparent diversity.

Augustine formulates this rule as follows: "In those places where things are used openly we may learn how to interpret them when they appear in obscure places" (*OCD*, iii, xxvi, 37). If we are attempting to understand what the word "shield" means in a given psalm, we must seek out its meaning in the other psalms. Augustine adds that one must not apply this rule blindly; the word may have more than one meaning, and a single meaning may be evoked by more than one word. We do not have here an assertion of the absolute

oneness of meaning, but only a tendency to control and re-
strict plurality (we shall return to this point).

To this first regulatory standard a second is added: not only
does the same word or the same sentence always have the
same meaning within a text, in principle, but the various
words or sentences of the text all have a single and common
meaning. The variety of signifiers is just as illusory as that of
signifieds. At bottom, the Bible endlessly repeats the same
thing, and if we do not understand the meaning of one passage we have only to look at the meaning of another: they are
the same. Origen had already formulated this axiom: "Let us
recognize that, Scripture being obscure, we must not seek
other means for understanding it beyond that of bringing
together the passages in which elements for exegesis are dispersed" (*Select. in Ps., Ps. 1*). Augustine follows him on this
point: "Hardly anything may be found in these obscure
places which is not found plainly said elsewhere" (*OCD*, II,
vi, 8); and so does Thomas Aquinas, who reformulates the
principle: "Nothing necessary for faith is contained under the
spiritual sense that is not openly conveyed through the literal
sense elsewhere."[2]

Concordances

By virtue of attempting to prove the unity of meaning and
text in this fashion, we are drawn into an endless task of
establishing intratextual relationships, or, to use the earlier
term, *concordances*—to such an extent that sometimes the
search for equivalences becomes a goal in itself. Augustine's
sermons provide a good example. Starting from the symmetrical positions occupied by Christ and John the Baptist, Augustine ends up with numerous and intricate resemblances
and oppositions in the texts that describe these two figures:
the former was born in the winter solstice, when the days

[2]*Summa Theologiae* (New York, 1964–76), I, qu. 1, a.10, r.1.

grow longer, the latter in the summer solstice, when the days grow shorter; Jesus was born to a young virgin mother, John to an elderly woman; the one was enlarged in death since he was raised up on the cross, the other was diminished, since he was decapitated, and so on (see Pontet, p. 141). It is clear that Augustine is even more attentive here to oppositions than to identities; thus it is no longer a matter of aiming to establish a unique meaning through the establishment of intratextual relationships (not immediately, in any case); the analysis frees itself for a moment from the too visible control exercised by the search for meaning.

The determined quest for concordances gives rise some seven centuries later to a specific heresy, that of Joachim of Floris. Joachim devoted all his energies to concordances in several works, one of which was even called *Livre de la concordance entre les deux Testaments.* Here we read the following:

> We say that concordance is, properly speaking, a similarity of equal proportions that is established between the New and the Old Testament.... So it is that in both texts a character corresponds to a character, an order to an order, a war to a war, and they face each other with parallel aspects ... in such a way that the meaning of things is partially unveiled, and the parallelism makes it possible to understand better what is said.... If our reasoning is correct, there are thus two signifying things for every thing signified.... [An example follows:] Concordance exists between Abraham and Zachary, to go back to one of our examples, because each of these men, in his old age, begets with his wife—who has been sterile until then—an only son. And let it not be said that there is dissimilarity here because the patriarch Isaac begat Jacob, whereas John did not beget Christ but baptized him: indeed, bodily begetting was confirmed in the former, who was the father of a people of flesh and blood, Israel; and in the latter spiritual begetting was affirmed, because he was the father of all Christian people according to the spirit.[3]

[3]*L'Evangile éternel,* vol. 2 (Paris, 1928), pp. 41–42.

Might we not be reading here a "structural analysis of myth"?

The heresy arises from the fact that the Old and New Testaments are situated on exactly the same level and that the latter's priority over the former—the very basis for patristic exegesis, as we shall have occasion to reaffirm later on—is thereby eliminated. To such an extent that Joachim is ready to interpret not only the Old Testament as announcing the New, but also the New Testament as announcing a third stage: the imminent end of the world. Instead of seeing a relation of accomplishment between the two Testaments, as the orthodox tradition would have it, we find ourselves dealing here with a simple repetition, with two nonhierarchical signifiers of a single signified. Joachim is quite explicit on this point:

> When you have discovered what the Old Testament signifies, you will not need to seek out the meaning of the New, for there can no longer be any doubt on this subject, their two meanings are one, and the two Testaments have a single spiritual explanation. [*L'Evangile éternel*, 2:45]

Joachim's exegetic practice, which was already incipient in certain of Augustine's texts, goes well beyond the categories of patristic exegesis; the inherent interest of Joachim's work, rather than its exemplary value, is what has held my attention here. What remains characteristic of Christian strategy is the *affirmation of the unity of meaning* of the Bible, and the control exercised over polysemy on that basis.

New Meaning or Old?

The biblical exegete has no doubt as to the meaning he will end up with. That is indeed the most solidly established point of his strategy: the Bible expresses Christian doctrine.

The work of interpretation is not what makes it possible to establish the new meaning, quite to the contrary: certainty concerning the new meaning is what informs interpretation. Origen could already proclaim that, in order to interpret Scripture properly, it is necessary (and sufficient) to know the divine message; conversely, for those who do not know this message, Scripture remains forever obscure. "Divine things are communicated to men somewhat obscurely and are the more hidden in proportion to the unbelief or unworthiness of the inquirer" (*On First Principles*, IV, i, 7).[4] "For in no other way can the soul reach the perfection of knowledge except by being inspired with the truth of the divine wisdom" (ibid., IV, ii, 7). Thus the end result is known in advance; what the exegete is looking for is the best way to get there. This is the very comparison Augustine uses: "If [the reader] is deceived in an interpretation which builds up charity, which is the end of the commandments, he is deceived in the same way as a man who leaves a road by mistake but passes through a field to the same place toward which the road itself leads" (*OCD*, I, xxxvi, 41). An interpretation that works in charity cannot be false.

This principle, cornerstone of patristic exegesis, is formulated repeatedly by all who practice this strategy. "For Irenaeus...," writes R. M. Grant, "there is one standard of correct interpretation. The standard is the rule of faith...." Clement of Alexandria asks, with respect to the senses in which Scripture can be taken: "How is the reader to choose among them? What guiding principle is to govern his interpretation? For one who was devoted to the Church there could be only one answer: Faith in Christ, in his person and in his work." For Tertullian, "the only way... to determine whether to interpret a passage literally or to allegorize it was to see whether or not its plain meaning was in accordance with the teaching of the Church" (Grant, pp. 72, 80–81, 107).

---

[4]Trans. G. W. Butterworth (New York, 1966).

Augustine frequently reformulates this idea:

You should make use of this opportunity to inform him [the candidate for conversion] that if he hears anything even in the Scriptures that has a carnal ring, he should believe, even if he does not understand, that something spiritual is therein signified that has reference to holy living and the life to be. Now this he learns in brief, so that whatsoever he hears from the canonical books that he cannot refer to the love of eternity, and truth, and holiness, and to the love of his neighbor, he may believe to have been said or done with a figurative meaning, and endeavor so to understand as to refer it to that two-fold love. [*The First Catechetical Instructions*, xxvi, 26, 50][5]

We know in advance that the canonical books speak of love; this knowledge thus provides us both with an index showing which expressions are endowed with secondary or symbolic meaning, and with the very nature of this meaning. The unknown in this undertaking is not the content of the interpretation, but the way in which the interpretation is constructed: not the "what" but the "how." This is what Augustine says in a shorter statement of the same rule: "In the consideration of figurative expressions a rule such as this will serve, that what is read should be subjected to diligent scrutiny until an interpretation contributing to the reign of charity is produced" (*OCD*, iii, xv, 23).

Since it is the "final" meaning that counts above all, we shall pay little attention to the "original" meaning or intention of the author. The search for such meaning is an almost harmful preoccupation, external to the exegetic project, which is to connect the given meaning to the new meaning.

Whoever finds a lesson [in the Scriptures] useful to the building of charity, even though he has not said what the author may be shown to have intended in that place, has not been deceived, nor is he lying in any way. [*OCD*, i, xxxvi, 40]

[5]Trans. J. P. Christopher (Westminster, Md., 1946).

And again:

> It is one thing not to see what the author himself thought, and another to stray away from the rule of piety. If both can be avoided, the reader's harvest is at its peak. But if both cannot be avoided, then, even if the author's intention may be uncertain, it is not useless to bring to the surface a deeper meaning, one in conformity with the true faith. [*De Gen. ad. litt.*, I, 21]

The search for intention is at any rate shifted to the background, behind the edification of charity and the "rule of piety."

The Doctrine of the Four Meanings

It has been generally agreed since the patristic period that Scripture has multiple meanings. The most common variant on this theme consists in saying that its meaning is quadruple, articulated first on the basis of an opposition between *literal* (or historical) meaning and *spiritual* (or allegorical) meaning, the latter being then subdivided into three categories: *allegorical* (or typological) meaning, *moral* (or tropological) meaning, and *anagogical* meaning. One of Aquinas's formulas codifies what had long been a widespread opinion, as follows:

> That first meaning whereby the words signify things belongs to the sense first-mentioned, namely the historical or literal. That meaning, however, whereby the things signified by the words in their turn also signify other things is called the spiritual sense; it is based on and presupposes the literal sense. Now this spiritual sense is divided into three. For, as St Paul says, *the Old Law is the figure of the New,* and the New Law itself, as Dionysius says, is *the figure of the glory to come.* Then again, under the New Law the deeds wrought by our Head are signs also of what we ourselves ought to do. Well then, the allegorical sense is

brought into play when the things of the Old Law signify the things of the New Law; the moral sense when the things done in Christ and in those who prefigured him are signs of what we should carry out; and the anagogical sense when the things that lie ahead in eternal glory are signified. [Pp. 37–39][6]

Let us begin by clarifying some terminological details. Moral meaning is also called tropological—a term that should be avoided here, so that there will be no confusion with "trope." "Allegory" sometimes designates the last three meanings taken together, sometimes only one of them; in order to avoid more confusion, we shall speak of spiritual meaning in the first case, of typological meaning or, more simply, of typology in the second—although this latter term is a modern one.

Now here is an example of an interpretation according to the four meanings, proposed by Dante in the famous— although perhaps inauthentic—letter to Can Grande:

That this method of expounding may be more clearly set forth, we can consider it in these lines: "When Israel went out of Egypt, the house of Jacob from a people of strange language; Judah was his sanctuary and Israel his dominion" [Ps. 114]. For if we consider the *letter* alone, the departure of the children of Israel from Egypt in the time of Moses is signified; if the *allegory*, our redemption accomplished in Christ is signified; if the *moral meaning*, the conversion of the soul from the sorrow and misery of sin to a state of grace is signified; if the anagogical, the departure of the sanctified soul from the slavery of this corruption to the liberty of ever-lasting glory is signified.[7]

[6]The classical treatment of the question of the four meanings is that of Ernst von Dobschütz, "Von vierfachen Schriftsinn. Die Geschichte einer Theorie," in *Harnack-Ehrung. Beiträge zur Dirchengeschichte* (Leipzig, 1921). The four volumes of Henri de Lubac's *Exégèse médiévale* explore all aspects of the question, but they are not easy to use. For a more succinct presentation in French, see André Pézard, *Dante sous la pluie de feu* (Paris, 1943), appendix viii, pp. 372–400: "Les quatre sens de l'Ecriture."
[7]In C. A. Dinsmore, *Aids to the Study of Dante*, (Boston, 1903), p. 267.

Here we see that one way of distinguishing the three spiritual meanings is to relate them to time: past (typological), present (moral), future (anagogical).

Christian Allegory?

One problem is still much debated in our day: that of the originality of Christian allegory with respect to contemporary or earlier pagan allegory, as it was practiced in particular in ancient Greece. One can guess what are the two competing theses: according to certain authors, the difference is purely substantive, an already-existing form (pagan allegory) having been applied to a new matter (Christian ideology); according to other authors, including several churchmen, Christian allegory is entirely different from pagan allegory, even in its forms.

Without going into too much detail, we may observe that the three spiritual meanings are brought forth on the basis of statements whose literal meaning is maintained: in other words, we are dealing with propositional symbolism. This observation is usually formulated as follows: the literal meaning has to be upheld. And very often, it is precisely in the maintenance of the literal meaning that we have seen the specificity of Christian allegory; pagan allegory in fact demands its abolition.

Thus Erich Auerbach writes:

> In [allegorism or symbolism], at least one of the two elements combined is a pure sign, but in a typological relation both the signifying and the signified facts are real and concrete historical events. In an allegory of love or in a religious symbol at least one of the terms does not belong to human history; it is an abstraction or a sign. But in the sacrifice of Isaac considered as a figure of the sacrifice of Christ, it is essential and has been stressed with great vigor, at least in the occidental tradition, that neither the prefiguring nor the prefigured event lose their

literal and historical reality by their figurative meaning and interrelation.[8]

And de Lubac:

> Two meanings which [as in Christian allegory] are added together, or two meanings of which the first, very real in itself although external, has simply to efface itself before the other or transform itself into the other on the basis of a creating or transfiguring event, are not two meanings which [as in Greek allegory] are mutually exclusive in the manner of appearance and reality, or "falsehood" and truth. No more indeed than the appearance or "falsehood" invoked in Greek mythology corresponds to the "letter" or to the "history" of Christian exegesis, does the truth of the former correspond, even from a *completely formal point of view,* to the truth of the second.... Very far from constituting the analogue, even an approximate one, then, to the Greek pairs to which we might be tempted to assimilate them, the Christian pairs constitute their *antithesis.* [2:517; emphasis added]

It is true that pagan allegory depends upon lexical symbolism. But that in no way proves the originality of Christian allegory: the latter is not the only one that depends upon propositional symbolism, which was perfectly familiar to the classical world, not only in practice—that goes without saying—but also in theory (as in the case of sign theory for Aristotle and the Stoics, or certain figures of thought such as the example, for the rhetoricians). The difference, if there is one, must be sought at a more specific level.

Typology

In order to circumscribe the question, let us go quickly back over the subdivision of spiritual meaning into three types.

[8]"Typological Symbolism in Medieval Literature," in *Gesammelte Aufsatze zur romanischen Philologie* (Bern, 1967), p. 111.

Moral meaning is the one that poses the fewest problems (so far as identifying it is concerned). It very closely resembles the form of thought that Aristotle described under the name of *example*[9]—and this resemblance holds good even for the examples of moral meaning he gave: a certain action of the past (of sacred history) has to be set in parallel with present actions, and has to serve as a guide to contemporaries in their interpretive work. Aristotle identifies two types: historical examples and nonhistorical (atemporal) examples, which in turn may be parables or fables. Here is a historical example: the war that the Thebans waged against the Phocians was evil; it follows that the Athenians should not wage war against the Thebans if they want to avoid evil; these two particular cases are related by a common property: the Thebans and the Phocians, like the Thebans and the Athenians, are neighbors (*Prior Analytics,* 69a). And here is a nonhistorical example: "Public officials ought not to be selected by lot. That is like using the lot to select athletes, instead of choosing those who are fit for the contest" (*Rhetoric,* II, 1393b). There is no formal difference here between classical antiquity and Christianity: from the standpoint of allegorical theory, the Theban war of Aristotle's example is equivalent to that of the children of Israel.

But typology remains to be characterized; for this is in fact what one usually has in mind in speaking of Christian allegory. Here is how typology is described by Augustine, whose work contains the seeds of the doctrine of the four meanings. The basic principle of this doctrine is announced as follows:

> For no other reason were all the things that we read in the Holy Scriptures written before our Lord's coming than to announce

[9]The term has a different meaning here from the one I gave it above, p. 75: in the preceding section, following Lessing's usage, I chose that term to designate the passage from the particular to the general, whereas Aristotle saw in the example the evocation of one particular by another—an evocation for which I myself used the term *allegory.* The same terms have been used in so many different senses that it is impossible to avoid verbal acrobatics in this area.

His coming and to prefigure the Church to be, that is to say, the people of God throughout all nations. [*The First Catechetical Instructions*, II, 6]

The same text presents several examples of typological exegesis:

In that people [the people of Abraham], without doubt, the future Church was much more clearly figured. [19, 33]

[Or again:] In all these things [all that happened to that people] there were signified spiritual mysteries closely associated with Christ and the Church, of which even those saints were members, although they lived before Christ our Lord was born according to the flesh. [ibid.]

[And also:] By the symbol of the flood, wherein the just were saved by the wood (of the ark) the Church to be was foreannounced, which Christ her King and God, by the mystery (of the wood) of his Cross, has buoyed up above the flood in which this world is submerged. [19, 32]

The Jewish people prefigure the Church, just as the flood announces its coming: here we have pronounced typological interpretations. Let us note that Augustine is not innovating here any more than he is elsewhere: typology was practiced by Saint Paul, from whom all of these examples are taken.

What exactly does typology consist of? Its features could be enumerated in the manner of historians of theology, going from the most general to the most specific as follows:

(1) It derives from propositional symbolism.

(2) It has to do with the *intersection* of properties, and not with exclusion or inclusion; in this sense, it stems from the Aristotelian example (from what I have been calling allegory).

(3) The two phenomena that constitute it belong to the past; they are both *historical* phenomena. That still does not suffice to characterize typology, however; indeed, historians of exegesis quote a sentence from Plutarch (*De Fortuna Alexandri*, 10) according to which the Homeric line "at once good

king and excellent warrior" not only praises Agamemnon, but also foretells Alexander's greatness. [10] Now that is a historical example, similar to Aristotle's, but not a typology, for although the events are repeated, one is not the accomplishment of the other.

(4) Only a specific relation between two phenomena allows us to speak of typology, within historical examples, and this relation does not appear in the rhetorical catalogues: it is the relation of *accomplishment*. There must be gradation between two phenomena in favor of the second: the first announces the second, the second accomplishes the first. As we have already seen, to put them on the same plane would be heresy, from the Christian viewpoint.

(5) The following restriction would apply purely to content: we shall agree to label *Christian* typology the one that is realized within the framework of this particular ideology. This restriction is required because of the fact that there exists a non-Christian typology, as Leonhard Goppelt has clearly shown.

(6) Finally, within Christian typology, we shall single out *testamentary* typology, according to which the events of the Old Testament announce those reported by the New Testament. This is what the "second" meaning (in the theory of the four meanings), the one designated above as "typology," refers to. This new restriction is necessary owing to the fact that the fourth meaning, the anagogical one, shares in certain properties of typology without being a testamentary typology. The anagogic meaning involves eschatology: on the basis of one series in which the Old and New Testaments are merged, we deduce another that is to come (the end of the world). The difference is twofold: we are dealing with prophecy, not with an interpretation of the past; and no text

---

[10]Quoted by Leonhard Goppelt, *Typos. Die typologische Deutung des Alten Testaments in Neuen* (Gütersloh, 1939), p. 20. Goppelt's book includes a brilliant treatment of the problems of typology.

plays the role here that the New Testament played with respect to the Old in testamentary typology.

If one were to define "typology" in such a way that it were not linked exclusively with Christian doctrine, one could observe the same "historical example of accomplishment" elsewhere. Without following up on this, I shall suggest that there is a great deal of "typology" in a major interpretive strategy of our time: psychoanalysis. Here the two events in question are no longer situated in the history of humanity but in that of the individual; it remains the case that the more recent phenomenon (for example, a neurotic symptom) is perceived as the "accomplishment" of an earlier act (infantile traumatism), which in turn "announces" the other.

Special Functions of Symbolic Expression

Symbolic expression having been discovered, then defined, then related to a secondary meaning, and this latter operation having been supported by proofs, the question remains: *Why was there a need for an expression other than direct expression* (expression through signs)? What functions is symbolic expression capable of taking on, beyond those that nonsymbolic expression can handle?

Let us raise the question by asking: What *can* the functions of symbolic expression be, in any case whatever? I shall identify two, to begin with, which for simplicity's sake I shall call "internal" and "external." First case: the reason for the symbolic lies in the very relation between symbolizer and symbolized: the symbolic expression is present because it *could not not be present.* Second case: the reason for the symbolic lies in the relation between symbol and its users, producers, or consumers; being *able* to choose between using it or not, they have *preferred* to use it, because of the supplementary advantages it offers: the reason for the symbol lies, then, in its effects.

Internal Functions

The first analysis is encountered infrequently in classical antiquity; however, isolated formulations can be found. The symbol is used, it is said, because one is speaking of ineffable things, such as divinity, by means of signs. For example, Strabo, in *Geographica* x, 3, 9: "The secrecy with which the sacred rites are concealed induces reverence for the divine, since it imitates the nature of the divine, which is to avoid being perceived by our human senses."[11] Origen: "There are certain things, the meaning of which it is impossible adequately to explain by any human language" (*On First Principles,* IV, iii, 15). Or Clement, *Miscellanies,* v, 4, 21, 4:

> All... who have spoken of divine things, both Barbarians and Greeks, have veiled the first principles of things, and delivered the truth in enigmas, and symbols, and allegories, and metaphors, and such like tropes. Such also are the oracles among the Greeks. And the Pythian Apollo is called Loxias [oblique].

Similar formulations come up in Maxim of Tyre, in the Emperor Julian, and, much later, in Dante (see Jean Pépin, *Mythe et allégorie,* pp. 268–271). Augustine, who concedes all sorts of functions to symbolic expression but who nevertheless has his preferences, uses an allegory to evoke the difference between the two sorts of expression, and thus the necessity of the narratives with symbolic content that fill the Bible. The comparison will be taken up again frequently and made explicit later on, especially by Hugh of St. Victor in his *Didascalion:*

> "On the zither and musical instruments of this type not all the parts which are handled ring out with musical sounds; only the strings do this. All the other things on the whole body of the zither are made as a frame to which may be attached, and

[11]Trans. H. L. Jones (London: Loeb Classical Library, 1917).

across which may be stretched, those parts which the artist plays to produce sweetness of song." Similarly, in the divine utterances are placed certain things which are intended to be understood spiritually only, certain things that emphasize the importance of moral conduct, and certain things said according to the simple sense of history.[12]

It is clear that, even here, there is immediate contiguity between allegorical narration and direct teaching, between recourse to symbols and to signs. Augustine has a hard time reserving an irreducible role for symbols, one that would be inaccessible to signs, as modern orthodoxy requires.

External Functions

The prevailing attitude in classical antiquity thus consisted in attributing to symbolic expression what has been called an external function, in justifying its presence solely by the *effects* that it produces on the users. This global function later found itself nuanced and subdivided, according to the various exegetic schools and tendencies.

The variant that is closest to the internal function is that of Maimonides in his *Guide for the Perplexed*. The nature of the revelation contained in the holy books is such that it cannot be revealed to men directly: it would blind them and they would not understand it.

> The Divine Will . . . has withheld from the multitude the truths required for the knowledge of God. . . . The subject being on the one hand most weighty and important, and on the other hand our means of fully comprehending those great problems being limited, He described those profound truths, which his Divine Wisdom found it necessary to communicate to us, in allegorical, figurative, and metaphorical language.[13]

---

[12]*The Didascalion of Hugh of St. Victor: A Medieval Guide to the Arts*, trans. Jerome Taylor (New York 1961), pp. 120–121.
[13]Trans. M. Friedländer (New York, 1910), pp. 3–4. (Translation modified.)

Allegorical expression is determined by the fact that men cannot understand revelations of this degree of seriousness in any other way; the internal function is embedded here, as it were, in an external function.

Augustine lists several varieties of external function:

> [The authors of the Holy Books] have spoken with a useful and healthful obscurity for the purpose of exercising and sharpening, as it were, the minds of the readers and of destroying fastidiousness and stimulating the desire to learn, concealing their intention in such a way that the minds of the impious are either converted to piety or excluded from the mysteries of the faith. [OCD, IV, vii, 12]

Three reasons can be identified here. The first (which does not often come up in Augustine) is that symbolic expression protects the divine word from contact with the impious; obscurity plays a *selective* role here, making it possible to set aside and to neutralize the uninitiated. The other two reasons, more frequently invoked, tend in opposite directions in certain respects.

One of them holds that symbolic expression is more difficult than nonsymbolic expression, and that it thereby adds an instructional task to its cognitive message. Clement of Alexandria had already said as much: "For many reasons, then, the Scriptures hide the sense. First, that we may become inquisitive, and be ever on the watch for the discovery of the words of salvation" (*Miscellanies*, VI, 15, 126, 1). Augustine stresses this point: "The obscurity itself of the divine and wholesome writings was a part of a kind of eloquence through which our understandings should be benefited not only by the discovery of what lies hidden but also by exercise" (OCD, IV, vi, 9), and: "But the language of the Word of God, in order to exercise us, has caused those things to be sought into with the greater zeal, which do not lie on the surface, but are to be scrutinized in hidden depths, and to be drawn out from thence" (*On the Trinity*, xv, xvii).[14] This difficulty, far from displeasing, attracts strong minds and spares them the tedium of direct expression; pride is at once conquered and flattered. "I do not doubt that this situation was provided by God to conquer pride by work and to combat disdain in our minds, to which those things which are easily discovered seem frequently to become worthless" (*OCD*, II, vi, 7). By means of which we are imperceptibly led to a reason apparently opposed to the preceding one: symbolic expression is preferable because it is more *agreeable*. For Augustine, difficulty is a source of pleasure:

No one doubts that things are perceived more readily through similitudes and that what is sought with difficulty is discovered with more pleasure. Those who do not find what they seek directly stated labor in hunger; those who do not seek because they have what they wish at once frequently become indolent in disdain. [*OCD*, II, vi, 8]

What is the precise reason for this connection between obstacles and pleasure, which brings to mind the satisfactions of watching a striptease?[15] Augustine declares that he does not know; but his pleasure is evident, as he manipulates utterances whose allegorical nature is not always apparent to us. The following rather long example makes this plain:

It may be said that there are holy and perfect men with whose lives and customs as an exemplar the Church of Christ is able to destroy all sorts of superstitions in those who come to it and to incorporate them into itself, men of good faith, true servants of God, who, putting aside the burden of the world, come to the holy laver of baptism and, ascending thence, conceive through

[14]In *Basic Writings*, trans. Whitney J. Oates (New York, 1948), vol. 2.
[15]Cf. *Theories of the Symbol*, trans. Catherine Porter (Ithaca, N.Y., 1982), p. 75.

the Holy Spirit and produce the fruit of a twofold love of God
and their neighbor. But why is it, I ask, that if anyone says this
he delights his hearers less than if he had said the same thing in
expounding that place in the Canticle of Canticles where it is
said of the Church, as she is being praised as a beautiful woman, "Thy teeth are as flocks of sheep, that are shorn, which
come up from the washing, all with twins, and there is none
barren among them?" [Cant. (Song of Sol.) 4:2]? Does one learn
anything else besides that which he learns when he hears the
same thought expressed in plain words without this similitude?
Nevertheless, in a strange way, I contemplate the saints more
pleasantly when I envisage them as the teeth of the Church
cutting off men from their errors and transferring them to her
body after their hardness has been softened as if by being bitten
and chewed. I recognize them most pleasantly as shorn sheep
having put aside the burdens of the world like so much fleece,
and as ascending from the washing, which is baptism, all to
create twins, which are the two precepts of love, and I see no
one of them sterile of this holy fruit. [*OCD,* ii, vi, 7]

However difficulty may be articulated with pleasure, it is
this type of reasoning that justifies symbolic expression, and
thus also the task of interpretation, from Augustine's
viewpoint as from that of all patristic exegesis. In speaking
through symbols, one says nothing different from what
would be said without them; their advantage lies in the way
they act on the mind of the receiver.

Possible Judgments on the Symbolic

Ambiguity in Judgment

Symbolic and interpretive activity being what it is, how is it
to be assessed? We have just seen that, for reasons that it is
hard for him to spell out, Augustine is attached to the interpretive undertaking itself; but a certain ambiguity is discern-
ible in the judgments that he passes on the respective results
of interpretation (allegorical meaning) and comprehension

(literal meaning)—an ambiguity that he attempts to master in parallel warnings against excesses in either direction: "Just as it is a servile infirmity to follow the letter and to take signs for the things that they signify, in the same way it is an evil of wandering error to interpret signs in a useless way" (*OCD*, III, ix, 13).

If there is ambiguity (but not contradiction), it is because the principles underlying the judgments concerning the two meanings have different sources.

On the one hand, for reasons inherent in the traditional concept of language as it is embodied especially in rhetoric from Cicero on, ideas (things) are preferred to words, and thus, among words, the most transparent ones are preferred, those that give the most direct access to thought. Now metaphors and allegories attract attention to themselves; they are therefore to be condemned. "The desire of a person seeking such clarity sometimes neglects a more cultivated language, not caring for what sounds elegant but for what well indicates and suggests what he wishes to show" (*OCD*, IV, x, 24). The elegance of indirect expressions has little weight over against the transparency of direct signs; that is also why "instructing" is superior to "moving," and still more so to "pleasing"; thus a simple style (stripped of metaphors and of other indirect expressions) is preferable to others (see *OCD*, IV, xii, 28, and xxv, 55).

Preferring the signified to the signifier leads, on the other hand, to placing spiritual meaning above literal meaning. To the general reasons that dictate this preference some purely Christian considerations are added, for spiritual meaning, as its name already suggests, makes common cause with the spirit, whereas literal meaning finds itself relegated to the rejected carnal, material side. Augustine states this quite explicitly:

> When that which is said figuratively is taken as though it were literal, it is understood carnally. Nor can anything more appro-

125

priately be called the death of the soul than that condition in which the thing which distinguishes us from beasts, which is the understanding, is subjected to the flesh in the pursuit of the letter. He who follows the letter takes figurative expressions as though they were literal and does not refer the things signified to anything else. [*OCD*, III, v, 9]

Between the two value judgments, there is obviously more of a disparity than a contradiction. The literal expression of a spiritual meaning is at the top of the hierarchy; then comes the spiritual meaning of allegorical expression, and only at the end do we find the literal (and carnal) meaning of that same expression.

Limiting the Proliferation of Meanings

A glance at the Christian tradition of biblical exegesis will allow us to expand upon and state precisely the significance of this ambiguity; for, in fact, not everyone shares Augustine's penchant for interpretation. Two tendencies are in confrontation—although once again they are not in direct contradiction.

The first, characteristic of any interpretive strategy, consists in restricting the proliferation of meanings, in seeking one meaning that is preferable to the others. The very nature of symbolic production and of its opposite number, interpretation, accounts for this first tendency. For to symbolize is nothing but to associate meanings; now all one has to do to associate two entities, is to predicate a common property for them (thereby obtaining metaphor), or else to position them as predicates of a single subject (as in metonymy); but are there any two entities for which the one operation or the other cannot be carried out? Nothing is easier than symbolizing and interpreting, and nothing is more arbitrary than a motivation. An interpretive strategy thus never seeks to open up paths which the mind would be unable to follow without this strategy, but seeks always and only to impose restrictions, to valorize certain semantic associations while excluding others. *Interpretive strategy proceeds by subtraction, not by addition,* or, to borrow Leonardo's terms, *per via di levare* and not *per via di porre:* whether through obligatory indices that trigger interpretation all by themselves, or through constraints bearing either on the interpreted segments, or on the motivation, or on the nature of the new meaning, and so on.

For this reason, at the heart of Christian tradition as with any other type of exegesis, we find defenders of the unique and literal meaning, opponents of symbolic polyvalence. Tertullian is an early witness to this; he opposes allegorical interpretation in the name of the principle of identity: "Now I wish that you would explain this metaphorical statement (translatio). . . . For you cannot possibly reckon both these corporeal subjects as co-existing in one person" (*Ad nationes,* II, 12). [16] Or, in Lactantius:

Anything that has actually taken place, anything that has been established by a clear material witness, cannot be converted to allegory; what has been done cannot not have been done, nor can the thing done deny its nature and take on a nature foreign to it. . . . What has taken place cannot be, as I have said, anything other than what has taken place, nor can what has been fixed once and for all in its own nature, in the characteristics belonging only to itself, escape into a foreign essence. [*Ad. nat.,* V, 38]

This attachment to literalism is found again and again throughout the history of Christian exegesis, although it only becomes dominant with the Reformation. "After 1517, when Luther definitely broke with the Roman Church, he ceased to

[16]In *The Writings of Quintus Sept. Flor. Tertullianus,* trans. Peter Holmes, The Ante-Nicene Christian Library, vol. XI (Edinburgh, 1869), p. 1:432.

make use of allegorization, and insisted on the necessity of 'one simple solid sense'" (Grant, p. 131). Another sixteenth-century exegete, John Colet, went so far as to write:

> In the writings of the New Testament, except when it pleased the Lord Jesus and his apostles to speak in parables, as Christ often does in the gospels and St. John throughout in the Revelation, all the rest of the discourse, in which either the Saviour teaches his disciples more plainly, or the apostles instruct the churches, has the sense that appears on the surface; nor is one thing said and another meant, but the very thing is meant which is said, and the sense is wholly literal. [Ibid., pp. 142–143]

In fact, this affirmation does not break entirely with the traditional attitude, for it is limited to the New Testament, which has never been the favorite field for allegorical exegesis.

The Inexhaustible Meaning of Scripture

We must note at once that numerous exceptions to this rule exist at the very heart of the Christian tradition. Saint John of the Cross, for example, affirms the fundamentally inexhaustible nature of the biblical text: "No words of holy doctors, albeit they have said much and may yet say more, can ever expound these things fully, neither could they be expounded in words of any kind."[17] The argument is based here on the ineffable nature of divine revelation; it will be similarly based, though in a very different spirit—that of an arithmetic combinatorial—in Saint Bonaventure's work. Scripture has its four meanings, naturally,

> but, like Ezekiel's "Living Creatures" [Ezek. 1:19], each of these four meanings also has its four sides, among which the varied content of its objects is distributed, so that we end up with

[17] *Spiritual Canticle*, trans. E. Allison Peers (Garden City, N.Y., 1961), preface, p. 230.

sixteen types of meaning in all. . . . On the other hand, if we divide the entire history of salvation into four periods (Nature, Law, Prophets, Gospel), we observe in each of these periods three mysteries, which makes twelve basic mysteries, corresponding to the twelve trees of Paradise. In each of these twelve hearths illuminated by intelligence all the planets are reflected, which allows us again to multiply by twelve and to obtain in this way the number 144, which is the number of the heavenly Jerusalem. [de Lubac, 4:268]

The Superiority of the Spiritual

But such mystical or scholastic exceptions to the principle of literalism are not what really counts. In a much more fundamental way, this principle is opposed and finally conquered by another, according to which the spirit is superior to the flesh. By transposition, we have to affirm the existence of spiritual meaning in order to be able to posit its superiority over carnal or literal meaning. No notion is more often repeated in Christian hermeneutics than Saint Paul's: "The letter killeth, but the spirit quickeneth" (2 Cor. 3:6). In this sense we may say that Christianity has a built-in need for allegorical interpretation: if there were no allegory, there would be no God (since it would be impossible to affirm the existence of a spiritual reality inaccessible to the senses and thus always a product of interpretation).

Nothing reveals the superiority granted to spiritual meaning over literal meaning better than the comparisons that characterize them both. "Jesus changes the water of the letter to the wine of the spirit," writes de Lubac (1:344). Richard of Saint-Victor compares "history to wood and allegory or mystical meaning to gold" (2:512). According to Augustine, Scripture is like "a plow of which it may be said that the whole thing works the soil, whereas properly speaking only the iron part penetrates" (4:97); and this "iron" corresponds to spiritual meaning.

More often than not, these comparisons do not stop at proclaiming the superiority of the spirit over the letter, but also attempt to base this superiority upon the opposition between *interior* and *exterior*. Allegory is the milk that must be extracted from the letter (4:183). Exegesis "unveils the spirit like the sun behind a cloud, like the marrow under the bone, like the seed under the straw" (1:308). Or like the honey in the comb, the nut in the shell (2:603). "For St. Cyril of Alexandria, Scripture was a garden full of delicate flowers: these flowers of spiritual meaning needed the protective envelop of leaves" (4:97). We are not far from the metaphor of cloak and body that has dominated theories of metaphor itself, throughout Western history.[18] The literal meaning is an envelope; the spiritual meaning is the thing itself.

To summarize: in spite of a tendency toward restriction, a natural tendency in any strategy, patristic exegesis has to postulate the existence of a meaning other than the literal. But this transcending of the literal is immediately checked and channeled into the doctrine of the four meanings, which at bottom, as Thomas Aquinas had already suggested, amounts to proclaiming the superiority of the spiritual meaning. This is expressed in an understated mode in one of Henri de Lubac's formulas, where he evokes "the oriented polyvalence of the symbol" (4:180) in Christian hermeneutics.

[18]Cf. *Theories of the Symbol*, chap. 2.

An Operational Interpretation: Philological Exegesis

My second example of interpretive strategy is both closely related to and quite remote from the preceding one. Remote from it because we are dealing now with a respectable modern science, philology, and not with an exegetic viewpoint that today appears wholly dependent upon an ideology circumscribed in time. But related to it as well, if only materially, since we can best attempt to grasp this new strategy at the moment when it makes its influence felt, and in a decisive way, upon the interpretation—again—of the Bible. Indeed, we shall study the principles of the new philological science in the work of an author who is revolutionary in the area of biblical exegesis: in Spinoza's *Tractatus Theologico-Politicus*.[1]

The Choice between Faith and Reason

The new method of interpretation Spinoza advanced is based upon a separation between faith and reason that he himself describes as "the main purpose of my whole work"

[1]Trans. R. Willis (London, 1862). The first edition appeared in 1670. The chapter is indicated in roman numerals, followed by a page reference to the English translation.

(XIV, p. 250). More explicitly, he seeks to prove that

> Scripture left reason absolutely free, and had nothing in common with, no dependence on, Philosophy, but that this as well as that must support itself on its own footing... [and] that each [revealed knowledge and natural knowledge] may possess its own province without clashing, and neither need be subordinate to the other. [Preface, pp. 27-28]

As this separation becomes the basis for the new exegetic method, it seems important to begin by sketching the rationale for it.

Two Types of Discourse

Spinoza develops his argument more or less as follows. An idea can be taught in two ways: by an appeal to reason alone, or by an appeal to experience. But the former approach can be practiced only with people who are very well educated and clear thinking. Such people are rare; therefore, if one wishes to reach the multitudes, it is preferable to draw upon experience (v, pp. 114-115). Now Scripture is in fact addressed to everyone and "the whole contents of the Bible are accommodated to the capacity and preconceived opinions of the vulgar" (xv, p. 259). But in what does this recourse to experience consist? In this: that Scripture presents doctrine in narrative form, and not through definitions and deductions. "And all its teaching to this effect, Scripture confirms by appeals to experience only in the histories of those whose laws and actions it records" (v, pp. 115-116).

So there are two types of discourse, which differ both in structure (one is deductive, the other narrative) and in function: the one serves to make truth known, the other to act upon the reader (since the primary function of these histories cannot be the transmission of truth: they achieve this indirectly and imprecisely). As for Scripture, it consists exclusively of this second type of discourse; as a result, its notional content is weak but its persuasive force is great. "From these facts it follows that the doctrine of Scripture contains no sublime speculations, no philosophical problems, but simple things only, that may be apprehended even by the dullest" (xii, p. 241). One further step consists in saying that one of these types of discourse is maintained within the limits of a representative function, whereas the other (that of the Bible) is exhausted in the action that it exercises:

> Men may teach and illustrate so much as is necessary to enforce obedience, and as suffices to impress the minds of those addressed with devotional feelings. [v, p. 116]

> Scripture was not intended to teach the sciences; whence we may see that it is obedience only which is required from man, and that stubbornness and contempt, not ignorance, are condemned. [xiii, p. 241]

One type of discourse has to do with the *ignorance/knowledge* pair, the other with the *submission/resistance* dyad.

The reader may have noticed the way in which Spinoza shifted ground in order to arrive at this conclusion. To establish his opening distinction, he had admitted that both types of discourse could serve to transmit truth, but that one was suited only to cultivated minds, whereas the other was good for the masses—whereas now only one type of discourse is recognized as capable of transmitting truth: the other is reserved to act upon the receiver, on the pretext that science cannot be taught to the uncultivated. Are we dealing here with two different modes of formulating truth, or rather with the opposition between truth and faith? Perhaps it is Spinoza's prudence that keeps him from adopting the second interpretation of his dichotomy without reservation. If it is accepted, however, it turns out to give rise to two homogeneous sequences, whose articulation is by no means absent

133

from our own discourse today. On the one hand, there is truth, knowledge, reason, philosophy, science; on the other, faith, effect on the receiver, and, as we say today, ideology. These two types of discourse are defined more or less formally: *scientific* discourse is that in which the representative function dominates the impressive function (if we may so label the function that has to do with the receiver); conversely, *ideological* discourse is that in which the impressive function is dominant.

The Dangers of Confusion

What counts for Spinoza is the separation of these two areas, and their apparent symmetry.

> [We] maintain unshaken the position, that theology is neither subject or subordinate to reason, nor reason subject to theology, but that each reigns supreme in its own proper sphere; the sphere of reason being truth and knowledge, whilst that of theology is piety and obedience. [xv, p. 264]

From there we pass directly to the interpretation of the Scriptures, and can deduce a first principle which is only an application of the basic dichotomy: we must not subject Scripture to reason any more than, conversely, we must subject reason to Scripture.

A historical figure illustrates each of these parallel dangers. The man who bent Reason to Scripture was called Alfakar (or Alpakhar); he was one of Maimonides' adversaries. "This Rabbi [Alfakar] maintained that reason ought to be not merely aidant, but subordinate, to Scripture" (xv, p. 260). More precisely, if one passage from the Bible contradicts another, clearer one, that suffices to enable us to decide that the former is metaphorical, and that it must therefore be subject to interpretation, even if Reason picks up no indication of this metaphoricity. So it is with the passages in which God is spoken of in the plural: "Wherefore all such passages are to be explained metaphorically; to wit, not because it is repugnant to reason to suppose that there are more Gods than one, but because Scripture itself directly affirms that there is only one God" (xv, pp. 260–261). Spinoza reproaches Alfakar not because the latter brings biblical texts into confrontation with each other, but because, once his reading is over, he refuses to use his reason to formulate judgments; because even in an area dependent upon Reason and no longer upon Scripture, the dominant position of the latter continues to be maintained. "It is true, indeed, that Scripture is to be interpreted by Scripture so long as the question is of the sense of the language, and the meaning of the prophets; but, having found the true sense, it is then indispensable that judgment and reason be summoned to approve of the conclusions attained" (xv, p. 261).

The two areas must be kept strictly apart. One may wonder whether Spinoza himself succeeded completely in this, for he wrote: "In the same way, there are very many expressions in conformity with the opinions of the prophets and the vulgar which reason and philosophy, but not Scripture, declare to be false or mistaken, although all must be supposed to have been true in the opinion of their authors, by whom reason and philosophy were little regarded" (xv, p. 263). Does not Spinoza himself regard "Reason" a little too highly? But what has happened is that he has shifted onto different ground. The question of the *meaning* of a text has to be strictly separated from that of its *truth* (we shall see this again later); this latter alone is the business of Reason and consequently one has no right to use Reason to establish meaning. Alfakar was establishing a falsehood, deducing from it the existence of a metaphor and changing the meaning of the utterance under examination; his error lay in this transition.

Maimonides himself represents the opposite danger.

He . . . maintained that we could never be certain of the truth of any one of these [interpretations], unless we knew that the particular part, interpreted as proposed, contained nothing

which either did not entirely agree with reason, or which was
seen to be completely repugnant to reason, for if the passage in
its literal sense were found wholly repugnant to reason, he
thought that the sentence required to be otherwise than literally
interpreted. [vii, p. 163]

Maimonides thus proceeds exactly as patristic exegesis had
done; the only difference is that in the place of "Christian
doctrine" we find "Reason": "doctrinal implausibility" is in
both instances the index of allegory and thus the trigger for
interpretation. The unformulated presupposition of this approach is that *the Scriptures cannot not speak the truth.*

Spinoza's objections parallel the ones he addressed to Alfakar, the two errors being reduced in effect to one, confusion
of what should be kept separate; but his argumentation is
more detailed. By subjecting Scripture to Reason, Maimonides implicitly admits that the object of Scripture is truth;
and, as a consequence, that it is addressed solely to cultivated minds. "If the opinion in question [Maimonides']
were correct, . . . the vulgar, as for the most part they either
ignore demonstrations, or do not appreciate them, could
know nothing of Scripture save from the explanations of critical philosophers" (vii, p. 164). Now everyone will agree that
Scripture is addressed to ordinary people and that as a result
it eludes the control of Reason. "For the matters that are not
susceptible of demonstration, and that form the greater bulk
of the Scriptures, could not be investigated satisfactorily on
such grounds as he proposes" [i.e., by Reason] (vii, p. 166).
Is it not absurd, then, to drag Reason onto a territory that is
not its own?

Meaning, not Truth

The exegetic distinction on which these separations depend
is the distinction between meaning and truth, which Spinoza
formulates very precisely:

Our business here is with the meaning only of the passages in question, nowise with the truth of what they state. Wherefore it is of prime necessity, whilst investigating the sense of Scripture, that we be not pre-occupied with our own views derived from or based on a knowledge of natural things (I say nothing here of our prejudices), lest we confound the true sense of the text with natural verity; the sense of Scripture being to be made out from the words of the text itself, or by legitimate reasoning upon them alone, no ground of induction being admitted but that which the text itself supplies. [VII, p. 146]

The objective of interpretation is the meaning of the texts alone, and interpretation is to achieve this goal without the help of any doctrine, whether true or false.

What Spinoza calls for is an interpretation without presuppositions, an interpretation directed solely by the text under analysis, and not by biases; he is thus calling for a scientific interpretation rather than a theological one. His "method requires nothing save natural light or understanding; for the nature and excellence of natural light consists especially in this, that it leads by legitimate deduction from things known or assumed as known to a knowledge of things obscure or unknown; nor is there any other concession which our method of inquiry demands" (VII, p. 161). The old hermeneutics postulated the existence of two sorts of texts: those in which meaning coincides necessarily with truth (alongside the sacred texts we can cite Homer), and those that have a meaning but not necessarily a true one. Theoreticians have devoted all their attention to the former class; the second has given rise only to practical techniques that have never become doctrine. Spinoza is apparently introducing very little that is new: he abolishes the separation between these two classes and declares that there are no texts whose meaning is necessarily true. This displacement of the frontier has crucial results, however: not only does one deal with the Bible as with any other text, but one becomes conscious of the techniques traditionally used in the interpretation of nonsacred texts, and one sets them up programmatically, taking their ideological implications for granted. One hundred fifty years later A. W. Schlegel, a theoretician of romanticism, will observe that "it is permissible to apply to Genesis the same rules for interpretation that have been adopted for countless other monuments of a remote Antiquity."[2]

The question remains whether it is always as easy as Spinoza seems to think it is to separate universal reason reduced to a pure logic from the particular reasons which threaten to tar interpretation with the brush of ideology, to separate *reason as method* from *reason as content:* whether it is always so simple to keep the one while getting rid of the other.

The Philological Project: The Science of Meanings

The starting point for interpretation, as Spinoza conceives of it, is an exact reversal of the fundamental principle of patristic exegesis. For the latter, the result of interpretation was given in advance (it was the text of Christian doctrine), and the only freedom one had was in choosing the path to follow between two fixed points: the given meaning and the new meaning. Spinoza, armed with his own separation between reason and faith and thus between truth (even religious truth) and meaning (of the holy books) begins by denouncing that other division:

> [Interpreters] mostly assume as the ground of all inquiry into the true meaning of the Bible, that it is everywhere inspired and literally true. But this is the very matter in debate, and should first appear from a careful examination and close criticism of the text; whereby, indeed, a right understanding of Scripture is much more certainly to be attained than by any amount of human gloss and gratuitous speculation. [Preface, p. 25]

[2]"De l'étymologie en général," *Oeuvres écrites en français* (Leipzig, 1846), 2:120.

Here, as earlier, Spinoza offers a critique of structure, not content: it is a question of changing not the nature of truth but its position. Far from being able to serve as the guiding principle of interpretation, the new meaning must be its result. One cannot seek an object with the aid of that object itself. The establishment of the meaning of a text has to be carried out independently of any reference to the truth of that text.

> Still, although the literal sense of the words is repugnant to natural reason, unless they be also clearly opposed to the principles and fundamentals of Scripture, this sense, viz. the literal sense, must be retained; and, on the contrary, if the expressions, literally interpreted, are seen to disagree with the principles derived from Scripture, although entirely accordant with reason and our natural understanding, they must be interpreted or taken metaphorically. [VII, p. 146]

New Constraints

This freedom concerning the meaning to be found will be counterbalanced by certain constraints destined to bear precisely upon that part of the interpretive task that patristic exegesis left free: that is, on the path between the two meanings, on the operations that allow us to pass from one to the other.

> Now on this point, in few words, I say that the proper method of interpreting Scripture does not differ from the proper method of interpreting nature, but agrees with it almost in every particular. For, inasmuch as the way of interpreting nature consists especially in bringing together, in arranging and contrasting, the facts of natural science, from whence, as from assured data, we arrive at general conclusions and definitions; so also in interpreting Scripture it is necessary to co-ordinate its simple statements and histories, and from them, as from fixed data and principles, to come to legitimate conclusions in regard to the meaning and purpose of the authors of the narrative. [VII, pp. 143–144]

The science of texts is assimilated by its method to natural science; the former proceeds like the latter, without any pre-conceived ideas, to the application of rigorous operations of verification and deduction, thereby arriving at the only truth that interests the interpreter, that of meaning.

More specifically, the quest will be subject to constraints of three orders: grammatical, structural, and historical.

In the first place, "Scripture history necessarily includes the nature and properties of the language in which it is written, and in which its authors were wont to speak" (VII, p. 145). The first requirement is thus linguistic in nature: in order to understand a text, it is necessary to understand the *language* of its epoch. No contradiction with "truth," that is, with dogma, authorizes us to attribute to a word any meaning that is not attested elsewhere in the language; and if linguistic usage did not allow us to attribute any other meaning to this word, there would be no other way to interpret the sentence (VII, p. 147). Which implies that words have, in principle, a single meaning, or at least that all their meanings belong to the lexicon; that is to say that there is no possibility of producing metaphors, of using words in a meaning that is not their own.

The second requirement has to do with the *coherence* of the text. Spinoza's point of departure is the very one that we have identified at the root of patristic exegesis: a text may not contradict itself, all its parts affirm the same thing. Spinoza for his part conceives of this study as the constitution of a series of thematic (paradigmatic) classes in which related segments are grouped. "The matters treated in each book must be noted and brought under distinct heads, so that a connected view of every passage which speaks of the same thing may be obtained, and the passages of doubtful or obscure meaning, or which contradict one another, may be known" (VII, p. 146). Once the principal truths have been established, the interpreter looks at the details, letting himself be guided by the principle according to which the text remains consistent with itself throughout. As a result, the index of secondary meaning, the trigger for interpretation, will be not doctrinal implausibility, as in patristic exegesis, but *in praesentia* contradiction. "That we may truly know therefore whether Moses believed God to be fire or not is by no means to be inferred from this, that such an opinion agrees with, or is repugnant to, reason, but solely from the other expressed opinions and views of Moses" (VII, pp. 146–147). This requirement of consistency accentuates anew the principle stated above: it is another reason why a word keeps the same meaning at all times. If the meaning of one sentence has been established, this meaning must be kept in mind in the interpretation of all the other sentences, whether or not they are already in harmony with reason (VII, p. 147).

The third group of constraints bears upon knowledge of the historical context.

> Finally, Scripture history ought to comprise an account of all the books of the prophets that have come down to us, the life, manners, and culture of the author of each particular book: who he was, on what occasion, at what time, to whom, and lastly, in what language he wrote; and then the fortune of the several books should be made known, viz. how and in what way each was first received, and into whose hands it fell; next, how many different versions of it are extant, by whose advice it was received among the number of the sacred books, and, lastly, how the books, all of which are now acknowledged as sacred, were gathered together into one body. [VII, pp. 147–148]

The "circumstances," or external evidence as to the meaning of a book, seem to be distributed here under three headings: the book in question, the author, and the reader. The book's destiny determines the degree of certainty that we may feel as to the establishment of the text. If it is indispensable to know the life and customs of the authors, this is because a determinism operates between man and book, and knowledge of the one helps us to know the other. "We the more readily explain the words of any one, as we are the better informed in regard to his genius and acquirements" (VII, p. 148). Knowledge of the reader is important too, for such knowledge determines the book's genre, chosen in terms of the audience for whom the book was written, and thus it supplies a key to decoding the text.

The search for circumstances never becomes a goal in itself; it is subordinate to a higher goal, which is understanding the text, establishing its meaning. It is not the text that enables us to know its author, but knowledge of the author that helps us to understand the text. This knowledge is indispensable in cases where the author's intention may change the meaning of the text as a whole, as with an ironic text, or one dealing with the supernatural. "It very often happens indeed that we read histories in different books, which in many respects resemble one another, but of which we form very dissimilar estimates, according to the opinion we entertain of the writers, or of the purpose of their writing" (VII, pp. 158-159). Ariosto's Roland, Ovid's Perseus and the Samson of the Bible singlehandedly massacre hosts of adversaries; Roland and Elijah fly through the air: but these acts take on different meanings owing to the fact that the intention of each author, as distinct from all the others, obliges us to come up with a particular interpretation: intention works like an indication of the key in which a piece of music is to be played. We are convinced of this "for no other reason than because we entertain different opinions of the writers of the several narratives" (VII, p. 159).

The True Meaning

All these techniques—linguistic, intratextual (or structural), historical—are necessary in order to reach the ambitious goal of interpretation as Spinoza sees it: the establishment of the true meaning (which is entirely different, as we have seen, from a meaning that conforms to *the* truth). To be sure, Spinoza takes some precautions: the meaning of a passage may be undecidable if there is a question of things that cannot be perceived which surpass the limits of human credibility (VII, p. 160, note), and which therefore cannot be governed by reason; or if the words are expressly used to say something other than what they ordinarily signify ("this indeed may be conjectured, but cannot be certainly deduced from the fundamentals of Scripture" [VII, p. 152]). But as a general rule—and this is our compensation, after the build-up of constraints that is so at odds with the operational flexibility of patristic exegesis—the meaning produced by interpretation is the only meaning, and the true one: "The method of investigation we have propounded, then, appears to be the true and only one... " (VII, p. 153).

On the Evolution of Philology

The label "philology" is ordinarily attached to activities that resemble Spinoza's in their objectives, but that are not institutionalized until later. The continuity of these two undertakings is nevertheless striking, and accounts for my anachronistic use of the term, provided that "philology" is understood as shorthand for philological exegesis (or interpretation). This continuity is perhaps established by actual transmission (with Richard Simon as intermediary), but also and especially by a profound similarity between the underlying positions. Continuity does not mean identity, however: the philological method evolved at the same time as its presuppositions. This will become apparent through a rapid examination of some representative texts of philology's triumphant phase, the nineteenth century.[3]

As in Spinoza's time, philology is defined by the rejection of the basic principle of patristic exegesis—namely, that meaning is given in advance—and by constraints that bear on mechanics alone. Given that the polemic Spinoza launched was victorious, the dispute has lost much of its relevance today. Nevertheless, August Boeckh still finds it necessary to write:

> It is completely ahistorical to prescribe that everything in the interpretation of Holy Scripture must be explained according to *analogia fidei et doctrinae;* here, the standard that is to guide explanation is not firmly established itself, for the religious doctrine born of the explanation of Scripture has taken very diverse forms. Historical interpretation has to establish uniquely what linguistic works mean; it is of little consequence whether they be true or false. [Pp. 120–122]

Meaning, not truth: this is indeed in the spirit of Spinoza.

The Unique Meaning

Proud of this renunciation of meaning dictated by a doctrine of reference, philology claims *objectivity* for the meaning it establishes; we no longer find meaning through truth, but

[3]I quote from the following texts: Friedrich August Wolf, "Darstellung der Altertumswissenschaft nach Begriff, Umfang, Zweck und Wert," in F. A. Wolf and P. Buttmann, ed., *Museum der Altertumswissenschaft,* vol. 1 (Berlin, 1807); F. A. Wolf, *Vorlesung über die Altertumswissenschaft,* vol. 1 (Leipzig, 1831); Friedrich Ast, *Grundriss der Philologie* (Landshut, 1808); Friedrich Ast, *Grundlinien der Grammatik, Hermeneutik und Kritik* (Landshut, 1808); August Boeckh, *Encyclopädie und Methodologie der philologischen Wissenschaften* (Leipzig, 2d ed., 1886); Gustave Lanson, *Méthodes de l'histoire littéraire* (Paris, 1925); Gustave Lanson, "La méthode de l'histoire littéraire," *Essais de méthode, de critique et d'histoire littéraire* (Paris, 1965). Joachim Wach's history, *Das Verstehen,* vol. 1, Tübingen, 1926, is not very useful if one has access to the primary texts. Ulrich von Wilamowitz-Moellendorf's *Geschichte der Philologie* (1921; Leipzig, 1959), is a history of knowledge about classical antiquity, not of the philological method. On the other hand, Peter Szondi's recent *Einführung in die literarische Hermeneutik* (Frankfurt, 1975) parallels my own study in many respects.

the truth of the meaning. From Spinoza on, this claim has been growing louder, but it has not changed its nature. F. A. Wolf rebels explicitly against the religious tradition that valorizes a certain plurality of meanings, *fecunditas sensus* (he seems to have in mind opinions like those of Saint John of the Cross), and he states:

> Two explanations that would concern the same passage, or two *sensus*, are never possible. Each sentence, each sequence of sentences has only one meaning, even if this meaning can be challenged. It may be uncertain; nevertheless, for someone who is seeking, there is only one. [*Vorlesungen*, p. 282]

> Furthermore it is necessary that each passage have only one *meaning*. . . . A certain meaning is presupposed for any discourse. [Ibid., p. 295]

One hundred years later, Gustave Lanson strikes a similar note as he transposes the philological method to the history of modern literature (he is of course not the first one to do this): "In all works of literature, even in poetry, there is one permanent and common meaning, which all readers must be capable of reaching, and which they must first propose to reach. . . . There is an accessible truth in literary studies, and that is what makes them noble and healthy" (*Méthodes*, pp. 41–42, 43).

If texts and sentences have only one meaning, that of words will likewise tend toward unicity. As Friedrich Ast puts it: "Each word has an original meaning from which the others derive" (*Grundriss*, p. 14). And Boeckh: "In a natural way a single meaning is at the root of every linguistic form and it is from this that one has to deduce all its different significations" (p. 94).

The True Meaning

If there is only one meaning, it must be possible to establish it with *certainty*, and there is no middle ground between fail-

ure and success. Hence a certain bombastic tone, especially noticeable in Lanson, who is sure not only that he has access to *the* truth, but that others have not found this truth. On the written page, one must find "what is there, all that is there, nothing but what is there" (*Méthodes*, p. 40). As it piles up certainties in this fashion, literary history progressively depletes its field of study:

> No one who has followed the trends in literary studies at all in recent years can have failed to notice that the area of disagreement is shrinking, that the realm of science, of uncontested knowledge, is spreading and leaves less room—unless they escape through ignorance—for the games of dilettantes, for the biases of fanatics; to such an extent that it is not illusory to predict a day when, having agreed on the definitions, content, and meaning of works, people will only argue over their goodness and their malice, that is, over their affective qualities. [Ibid., p. 36]

Unlike the literary historian, the critic invents his interpretations—which are necessarily false, since there is only one true one. In so doing, he substitutes his own wanderings for the writer's thought. The literary historians' creed is at the opposite pole: "We wish to be forgotten, we want only Montaigne and Rousseau to be seen, just as they were, as anyone will see them who applies his mind faithfully, patiently to the texts" (Lanson, *Essais*, p. 47). And the critic who has ideas is not to be contrasted with the hardworking philologist: as Lanson retorts, in an emblematic pronouncement: "We too want ideas. But we want true ones" (*Essais*, p. 53). In the face of this *credo*, one might well have maintained that to want true ideas is not to want any at all (or in Nietzsche's terms: "To renounce false judgments would be to renounce life itself, would amount to denying life").

This single and scientifically guaranteed meaning coincides with the author's *intention*. As Wolf says: "Hermeneutics is the art of grasping writers, and consequently the written

146

thoughts of another person—or even those expressed only orally—just as he has grasped them himself" (*Vorlesungen*, p. 271). Lanson's position is more nuanced in this instance: even if no objective meaning exists for a text (a supposition that he advances in his later writings), not all subjective meanings are situated on the same level: "It would perhaps not be exaggerating to suggest that the author's meaning is a privileged meaning all the same, one to which I may pay special attention" (*Méthodes*, p. 42).

Interpretation as Servant

Up to this point, the differences between Spinoza and the philologists are only quantitative; but the very position of philological technique in the two instances marks a deeper transformation. Let us recall the hierarchy that arose in Spinoza's work: his initial objective, which was inscribed in a tradition of biblical exegesis, is the establishment of the meaning of the text; to this end, he uses auxiliary techniques (linguistic, structural, historical). This hierarchy is reversed in the later tradition: *the principal objective becomes historical knowledge of a culture,* and this knowledge may rely upon auxiliaries other than textual interpretation. With respect to hermeneutics, philology moves little by little from the position of servant to that of mistress.

It is interesting to observe the different stages of this reversal. The transition point may be located in Ast, whose text remains ambiguous in this respect; he subordinates the interpretation of works to knowledge of the author's spirit; but that spirit, on the other hand, turns out to be made up of the works themselves!

Philology is the study of the classical world in the totality of its life—artistic and scientific, public and private. The center (*Mittelpunkt*) of this study is the spirit of Antiquity, which is reflected in the purest manner in the works of the ancient writers, but which also leaves its traces in the outward and particular life of the classical peoples; and the two elements of this center are the arts, the sciences, and the external life or content on the one hand, and representation and language, or the form of the classical world on the other. [*Grundriss*, p. 1]

Works are only reflections and traces of the spirit, but the spirit in turn is made up of works: the reflection is nothing other than object reflected itself.

In Wolf, the ambiguity disappears; the object and its reflection are no longer identical.

> The separate acquisitions that have been mentioned are at bottom only preparations for the one in question now, and all the ideas developed to this point converge toward this chief goal as toward a center. But this goal is nothing other than knowledge of ancient humanity itself, through the observation of an organically developed and meaningful national formation; this observation is conditioned by the study of ancient remains. ["Darstellung," p. 124–125]

Knowledge of works ("remains") is subject to that of national formation, which in turn is only a means for knowing ancient humanity.

Thus Lanson, when he formulates the objective of literary history, can now refrain from mentioning the fact that it aims at the interpretation of works (this activity is entrusted to a subordinate technique, that of textual explication).

> Our task consists . . . in preserving, filtering, evaluating everything that can contribute to forming an exact representation of the genre of a writer or of the soul of an epoch. [*Méthodes*, p. 34]

> Our higher function is to lead those who read to recognize in a page of Montaigne, in a play by Corneille, even in a sonnet by Voltaire, moments of French or European human culture. [*Essais*, p. 33]

148

The philological reading of a page no longer aims at the establishment of its meaning; that page is only a means of access to an individual, a time, a place. Textual interpretation is simply one of the tools available to the history of mentalities.[4]

Methods of Interpretation

The forms of philological inquiry have evolved as well. Wolf points out parenthetically, as it were, that interpretation may be "grammatical, rhetorical, and historical" ("Darstellung," p. 37). In the *Vorlesungen*, he proposes a different distribution: "interpretatio grammatica, historica, philosophica" (p. 274). The constants are thus grammatical and historical interpretation; the first establishes the meaning of sentences in themselves; the second, that of utterances, that is, of sentences taken in context (this is the difference between language [*langue*] and discourse [*discours*]). The distinction is illustrated by the example of a letter discovered by chance: "If someone finds in the street a letter whose words are very clear, he will still be unable to understand it fully, for he does not know the immediate circumstances concerning the person who wrote it or the person to whom it is addressed" (ibid., p. 294). He will understand the grammatical meaning (that of the sentences) but not the historical meaning (that of the utterances). As for philosophical interpretation, that seems to be a concession on Wolf's part to interpretations of the patristic variety. "After the meaning has been developed grammatically and historically, I may ask: how is this idea in conformity with truth?" (ibid., p. 275). The first two interpre-

[4]One may protest that the object of what is called philology has always been global historical knowledge and not the interpretation of texts, and that philology as such, for this reason, has not changed. But such an objection would only displace the problem: why is it precisely philology, and not hermeneutics, which becomes constituted during this period as an autonomous and influential discipline?

tations seek the meaning of the text, the third judges its truth-fulness; that is why, Wolf adds, "it is important for religious writings" (ibid.).

A disciple of Schelling and of Friedrich Schlegel, Ast be-longs among those theoreticians who see everything in terms of the triad consisting of a given thing, its opposite, and their synthesis. As far as texts are concerned, they have both (lin-guistic) *form* and *content* or being; the synthesis of the two gives the *spirit*. "Every life and every truth consist in the spiritual unity of being and form. . . . Being and form are the plurality in which the spirit is revealed; the spirit itself is their unity" (*Grundriss*, p. 3). "We call spirit the original unity of every being" (*Grundlinien*, p. 174).

As a result, there are three types of interpretation, and only three.

> That is why understanding of the ancient writers has three forms:
> 1. *historical*, with respect to the content of their works, which may be either artistic and scientific, or ancient in the broadest sense of the word;
> 2. *grammatical*, with respect to their form or language, and to their exposition;
> 3. *spiritual*, with respect to the spirit of the individual author and that of all Antiquity. The third understanding, the spiritual one, is the true one, and the highest, the one in which the historical and grammatical understandings interpenetrate, for a unified life. Historical understanding recognizes what (*was*) the spirit has formed; grammatical understanding recognizes how (*wie*) the spirit has formed it; spiritual understanding leads the what and the how (*was und wie*), matter and form, back to their original and unified life in the spirit. [*Grundlinien*, p. 177]

Spiritual interpretation is not independent; it is rather the unification, and thus the fulfillment, of the two preceding methods.

The similarity of the terms that designate the forms of understanding in this context and those that designate the meanings of Scripture in patristic strategy might lead us to see the former as a simple metamorphosis of the latter. Does not the subdivision into form, content, and spirit recall one of the earliest formulations, Origen's in *On First Principles,* where he wrote: "Just as man is made up, it is said, of a body, a soul and a spirit, so too is holy Scripture, which has been given for man's salvation by the generosity of God" (iv, 2, 4)? But if we examine the content of these distinctions in someone like Ast, we see the vast distance that separates them. In patristic exegesis, the *meaning* was historical; in philology, what is historical is the *method* leading to the discovery of meaning. In the one case the results of interpretation are codified, in the other its techniques.

It is in Boeckh that these subdivisions are established in the greatest detail and with the most painstaking articulation:

What is essential for understanding and for its manifestation, exegesis (*Auslegung*), is consciousness of what conditions and determines the meaning and signification of what is communicated or transmitted. We find here first the objective significa-tion of means of communication, that is, within the limits that are ours, of language. The signification of what is communi-cated will be determined first by the meaning of words in them-selves, and thus can be understood only if one understands the entire set of common expressions. But whoever speaks or writes uses the language in a particular and special way; he modifies it according to his own individuality. In order to understand someone, then, one must take his subjectivity into account. We use the term *grammatical* for a linguistic explana-tion made from the objective and general point of view, and *individual* for the one made from the viewpoint of subjectivity. The meaning of the communication is, however, further con-ditioned by the real circumstances in the course of which it was produced and knowledge of which is presupposed in those to whom it is addressed. In order to understand a communication, one must put oneself in the receivers' place in the given circum-stances. A written work, for example, receives its true meaning only when it is related to the prevailing ideas of the period in which it was created. We call this explanation by means of the real environment (*Umgebung*) historical interpretation.... Historical interpretation is closely linked to grammatical interpretation, in that it tries to find out how the meaning of words in themselves is modified by objective circumstances. But the individual aspect of communication is also modified by *subjective* circumstances, under the influence of which it is produced. The latter determine the direction and the goal of the communicator. Goals of communication held in common by more than one person do exist; this gives rise to certain genres, in language the genres of discourse. The character of poetry and prose lies outside of their differing styles, in the subjective direction and in the goal of representation. The individual goals of particular authors are located within these general distinctions: they form subdivisions of the broader genres. The goal is the ideal higher unity of what is communicated, a goal which, posited as a norm, is a rule of art, and as such always appears imprinted within a particular form, a *genre*. The exegesis of communication based upon this aspect will be designated at best, for this reason, as a *generic* interpretation; it is attached to individual interpretation in the same way that historical interpretation is attached to grammatical interpretation.... Hermeneutics is:

1. Understanding of what is communicated on the basis of the *objective* conditions:
a) on the basis of the meaning of the words *in themselves*—*grammatical* interpretation;
b) on the basis of the meaning of the words *in relation to* the real circumstances—*historical* interpretation.
2. Understanding of what is communicated on the basis of the *subjective* conditions:
a) on the basis of the subject *in himself*—*individual* interpretation;
b) on the basis of the subject *in relation to* the subjective circumstances, which lie in the goal and in the direction—*generic* interpretation. [*Encyclopädie,* pp. 81–83]

The four forms of interpretation according to Boeckh stem from a matrix based upon two oppositions: subjective vs. objective, and "isolated" vs. "in relation to a context": they might be rewritten as follows:

	ISOLATED	IN CONTEXT
OBJECTIVE	grammatical	historical
SUBJECTIVE	individual	generic

Wolf's philosophical interpretation has disappeared, having arisen from a different exegetic principle; one may suppose, on the other hand, that generic interpretation recaptures what Wolf designated by the term "rhetoric" (although he was not at all explicit on that point). Ast's spiritual interpretation is likewise missing, doubtless because it is not situated on the same plane as the others, but encompasses them all. The reader will have noted the extent to which Boeckh's suggestions remain current, in terms of interpreting genres as communication contracts, for example, or including the historical context *within* the meaning of the text, and so on.

Lanson pays much less attention to the way the various philological techniques are articulated, but his work offers a suggestion tending in this direction nonetheless: "The meaning of words and expressions [will be established] by the history of the language, grammar, and historical syntax. The meaning of sentences by the clarification of obscure relationships, historical or biographical allusions" (*Essais*, p. 44). Grammatical and historical interpretations are modeled on the syntagmatic dimensions of the interpreted segments, words or phrases (rather than on language and discourse). The devices enumerated in the following somewhat ironical list refer likewise to these two types of interpretation:

> Manuscript study, collation of editions, discussion of authenticity and attribution, chronology, bibliography, biography, search for sources, sketches of influence, history of reputations and of books, analysis of catalogues and dossiers, versification statistics, methodical lists of observations on grammar, taste and style, and how much else? [*Méthodes*, pp. 34–35]

In order to obtain an overview of the evolution of the philological subdivisions and thus of the concepts touching upon diversity of meaning, we can attempt to bring together in a single chart the various distributions summarized here. This is not without its dangers: the same words do not cover the same realities, and the latter may be evoked, conversely, under different names; furthermore, as we have seen, the articulations between concepts vary, thus the very meaning of the concepts does too. Nevertheless, let us hazard this chart of interpretive methods, which will give us an overview of the evolution of philology:

SPINOZA	WOLF	AST	BOECKH	LANSON
grammatical	grammatical	grammatical	grammatical	grammatical
structural				
historical	historical	historical	historical	historical
			individual	
	rhetorical		generic	
		spiritual		

Even if certain relationships are forced, one conclusion is clear: the form of interpretation that disappeared after Spinoza's day is the one called structural or intratextual, that is, the study of the text's internal consistency. The only later form that can be compared to it is Ast's spiritual interpretation. But the handful of common features do not allow the one to be assimilated to the other. With Spinoza, it is a question of establishing relationships between the various segments of the text, of searching for contradictions and convergences. With Ast, spiritual interpretation caps the two others, it combines in one all the results of the interpretations undertaken separately; it is not at all a question of confronting segments of the text among themselves. Ast, to whom we owe the most popular formulation of the "hermeneutic circle," is not indifferent to the problem of consistency; but he is thinking only of the relation between part and whole, not of the relation Spinoza theorized between part and part. Thus in Ast's work there is no trace of the techniques Spinoza proposed.

The evolution of what I call philology, from Spinoza to Lanson, is clear: the various changes all tend in the same direction. The hierarchical overturning of exegesis by its subordinates goes hand in hand with the disappearance of "structural" interpretation. *The chief victim of this evolution is intratextual analysis:* first dethroned from its dominant position and relegated to an auxiliary role, the search for the meaning of the text no longer receives much attention, and as a result its practice is abandoned to empiricism (to *explication de textes*), while theory fails to take over the elaboration of its techniques.

Now—and this is one of the somewhat surprising lessons of this historical promenade—no internal reason obliged philology to exclude intratextual analysis: the fact that the various techniques are found side by side in Spinoza is proof, if proof is needed. "Grammatical," "historical," and "structural" requirements all belong to the same family: they are constraints exercised on the operations to which the text is subjected in the search for its meaning. None of these constraints determines in advance, as the basic principle of patristic exegesis did, the direction in which the search itself must be oriented.

A Critique of Philology: Schleiermacher

We must not abandon this chapter of our history without looking at a critique brought to bear on several of the philological principles just summarized, right at the time of their earliest formulation. I am referring to Schleiermacher's doctrine, which belongs historically to the period we are examining (he had attended Wolf's courses, whereas Boeckh

attended Schleiermacher's) but which transcends it concep-
tually and, instead of illustrating a particular strategy of interpretation, constitutes one of the contributions to a general
theory of interpretation and of the symbolic to which I referred several times in Part One.[5]

Homogeneity of Meaning

Schleiermacher is already criticizing the very idea of sub-
dividing interpretation into grammatical and historical (or
any other) categories. For, according to him, such categories
constitute different *sources*, which contribute to the establishment of *a meaning*, but they in no way lead to different
meanings. The belief that there are separate meanings—
literal, historical, and philosophical—is an undesirable inher-
itance from the particular strategy of interpretation that we
know as patristic exegesis. Whatever means may be used to
establish the meaning of a text, that meaning always remains
of the same type, and there is no reason to bring categories
based upon differences in technique into hermeneutics.

> However correct the thing may be, I should nevertheless like to
> protest against that expression which always creates the illu-
> sion that historical and grammatical interpretation are each
> quite definite things. . . . [The philosopher-interpreter] can have
> been thinking of one thing only: that in a correct interpretation
> all the different elements must harmonize in the same single
> result. [Pp. 155–156]

Meaning does not vary according to the means used to establish it. On the other hand, it is appropriate to introduce a
distinction that arises from Schleiermacher's own idea of the

---

[5]I quote Schleiermacher's texts in translation from H. Kimmerle's edition of
Hermeneutik (Heidelberg, 1959). A few of the passages in question have appeared in French in Peter Szondi's useful study, "L'herméneutique de
Schleiermacher," *Poétique*, 1 (1970), 141–155, reprinted in his *Poésie et poétique
de l'idéalisme allemand* (Paris, 1975), pp. 291–315.

nature of his object. Meaning, for him, exists only in a process of *integration;* the act of interpreting (taken in a broader sense than the one in which I have been using this term) consists in being able to include a particular meaning in a larger whole. The isolated word is not yet the object of interpretation (but only of comprehension, we might say); interpretation begins with the combination of several signifying elements. Now a signifying fragment, a sentence, may be included within different frameworks: this position leads to a new subdivision whose resemblance to the one produced by philologists of the same period is purely superficial.[6]

Grammatical and Technical Interpretations

There are two principal contexts into which any given utterance may be integrated; consequently, there are two forms of interpretation for each text—Schleiermacher calls them *grammatical* and *technical* (the terms seem to be inherited from the exegetic tradition—Flacius's *Clavis* [1567]—but Schleiermacher alters their meaning). It would not be misleading to

[6]At least as far as the texts quoted above are concerned. On the other hand, Ast, for example, occasionally adopted a different perspective, one that closely foreshadowed Schleiermacher's. Alongside his categorization into form, content, and spirit, he proposes another, among the letter, the meaning, and the spirit of the text. "Spirit" remains the same in the two categorizations; but "letter" includes grammatical as well as historical interpretation. The hermeneutics of meaning is thus added to the earlier ones, and is nothing other than the "explanation of the meaning of a segment in its relations" (*Grundlinien,* p. 195). Thus the meaning of a given sentence will be different according to the contexts into which it is integrated: "The meaning of a work and of particular segments (*Stelle*) derives notably from the spirit and the orientation of the author; only someone who has grasped these and has familiarized himself with them is in a position to understand each segment in the spirit of its author (*Verfasser*) and to discover its true meaning.

"For example, a segment from Plato will usually have a different meaning from that of another segment, belonging to Aristotle, in which the meaning and the words might be almost the same.... Thus not only does a single word have different meanings, but so do specific similar segments, if their connections are different" (ibid., pp. 195–196). It is this same idea of the importance of connections that dominates Schleiermacher's thinking.

take the first as inclusion based on reference to collective memory (the paradigmatic context), the second as inclusion based on reference to the syntagmatic context. In the first case, the utterance is explained by recourse to global knowledge of the language; in the second, by reference to the discourse to which the utterance belongs, whatever the dimentions of this discourse may be. Here is the clearest formulation of the dichotomy: "The principal point of grammatical interpretation lies in the elements through which the central object is designated; the principal point of technical interpretation lies in the overall continuity (*Zusammenhänge*) and its comparison with the general laws of combination" (p. 56). On the one hand, isolated elements are confronted with the inventory of available elements (language); on the other hand, these elements are studied in their combination (discourse) and are compared to other types of combination. The two major rules of interpretation stem from this:

> First law: everything that, in a given discourse, must be determined more precisely must be so determined only on the basis of the linguistic space common to the author and his original public. . . . Second law: the meaning of each word, in a given passage, must be determined on the basis of its insertion into an environment. [Pp. 90, 95]

This fundamental opposition entails several others. Inscription within a paradigm is profoundly negative: it is the choice of one meaning to the exclusion of all others. Inscription within the syntagm, on the contrary, is positive: it involves taking a position inside a combination with other copresent elements. "There are two sorts of determinations of meaning: exclusion on the basis of the global context, and determination of position (*thetisch*) on the basis of the immediate context" (p. 42). "Determination on the basis of the broad [environment] tends to be exclusive; determination on the basis of the immediate environment is rather one of position" (p. 66).

The broadest discursive context is not the individual text but the entire work of a writer; that is why opposition between grammatical and technical interpretations can be conveyed in these other terms: language and author. Schleiermacher says as much in countless formulations:

> P. 56: Understanding in speech and understanding in the speaker (*Sprache, Sprechenden*).... Forgetting the writer in the grammatical and the language in the technical. To the extreme limit. P. 80: As this utterance has a double relation to the totality of the language and to the total thought of its author: thus, all comprehension consists in two phases, understanding the utterance as an excerpt from the language, and understanding it as a phenomenon in the one who is thinking. P. 113: Grammatically. Man disappears with his activity, and appears only as an organ of language. Technically. Language disappears with its determining power and appears only as an organ of man at the service of his individuality, just as, in the other case, personality was at the service of language.

From this it follows, among other things, that anonymous writings, such as myths, are not open to technical interpretation: we do not know with what we should integrate them: "There is no technical interpretation for the myth, for it cannot stem from one individual" (p. 85).

We would be entirely in error if we believed that technical interpretation consisted in looking for the man through the work. Schleiermacher's overall project, like Spinoza's, is to *subordinate all techniques to the search for meaning*—even while establishing meaning through integration into a higher framework—; thus there is no question of using the text in order to know its author, but rather of using the author to know the text. Furthermore, the *author* is specifically identified as a set of texts (of whatever nature): *as a syntagmatic context*. Any attempt to explain the texts through the life of their author is bound to fail. "With men as well known as Plato and Aristotle, does all that we know of their life and relations explain to us to the slightest extent why one followed a certain path in philosophy and the other another?" (p. 150). There follows a rejection of the privileged role allotted (in the framework of philological interpretation) to the author's intention, to the meaning that the author himself wanted to give his text; the writer is even particularly blind to some aspects of his own work, of which he is necessarily unconscious—unless he transforms himself, in turn, into a reader of his own works (but then, his interpretation is only that of a reader). Pp. 87–88: "Since we have no immediate knowledge of what is in him, we have to attempt to bring to consciousness what might remain unconscious for him, unless, upon reflection, he were his own reader." P. 91: "We [understand] the creator better than he understands himself, because many things of that sort are unconscious in him, which must become conscious in us." In this Schleiermacher picks up on an idea of his friend Friedrich Schlegel, who wrote: "*To criticize* means to understand an author better than he has understood himself" (*Literary Notebooks*, 983).

Fundamental Meaning, Specific Meaning

The intentional meaning is not privileged; which does not mean that one segment has an infinite number of meanings, or that all interpretations are equally welcome. Schleiermacher's position on this point is nuanced. It is only in a paradigmatic perspective that one can speak of the original and essential unity of the word. Now the global meaning is determined by the intersection of the two perspectives, paradigmatic and syntagmatic; and it is exceptional, if not impossible, for the original unity, the fundamental meaning, to coincide with the meaning as it is realized in a particular context.

> Every usage is particular, and the essential unity is mingled with what derives from chance. The essential unity thus never

appears as such. Therefore one cannot determine a particular use, in a given case, on the basis of another particular use, because of the presupposition that that implies. [P. 61]

The unity of the word is a schema, a nonsensical viewpoint. A given use *must* not be confused with the meaning. Just as the word is affected by the modification of its environments, so too is its meaning. [P. 47]

This attack goes directly against one of the axioms of patristic exegesis that we found again in the philologists: that of the unity of meaning, and thus of the possibility of explaining the meaning of one occurrence of the word by that of another. The fundamental meaning of the word is a construction of the mind; it is not found in any one utterance more than in another.

But if we must not expect to observe the fundamental meaning within a particular utterance, that does not mean that each utterance does not have a *unique* meaning. We are not to project the properties of language onto discourse any more than we are to set up syntagmatic meaning as a paradigmatic meaning. Words are polysemic out of context; but in a particular utterance, they take on a specific meaning. It is for that reason that Schleiermacher refuses to grant a special status to metaphorical expressions. The illusion of a metaphorical meaning that would be unlike the others stems from the fact that a discursive phenomenon is being examined with instruments appropriate to language. Within the utterance, words have a fixed meaning which is always of the same nature; it is only the confrontation of the meaning of the utterance with that of its constituent elements, thus of the discursive meaning with the linguistic meaning, that creates the impression of a transposition of meaning. "Words taken in the figurative sense keep their own precise meaning and only achieve their effect through an association of ideas on which the writer relied" (p. 59). "If we look more closely, the opposition between proper meaning and improper meaning disappears" (p. 91).

It is the same with entire texts: there exist no allegorical texts that would be different from other ones:

> If a segment is to be understood allegorically, the allegorical meaning is the sole and simple meaning of the segment, for the segment has no other; if someone wanted to understand it historically, he would not reproduce the meaning of the words, for he would not leave them with the meaning that they have in the continuity of the segment; just as if one were to interpret allegorically a segment that is supposed to be understood in another way. [P. 155]

To find the literal meaning of an allegorical passage is to find the meaning of the elements that constitute it, without taking their combination into account. Now meaning is determined by the combination to which it belongs; it is thus erroneous to consider it as indecisive and arbitrary.

It remains the case that the combinations to which a linguistic element may belong are *infinite* in number; thus meaning itself is infinite; and interpretation is an art (as Friedrich Schlegel was already saying: "Philology is an *art* and not a science").

> Interpretation is an art. For everywhere there is construction of what is finite and determined on the basis of what is infinite and indeterminate. Language is infinite because each element may be determined by the others in some particular way. It is the same with psychological [interpretation]. For everyone's individual outlook (*Anschauung*) is infinite. [P. 82]

Hermeneutic rigor is not transformed here into a positivistic scientism.

Some Historical and
Typological Conclusions

I should like to raise a question, in conclusion, about the historical significance of the opposition that I have proposed between patristic and philological exegesis. This confrontation between two approaches, singled out from among so many others, may seem arbitrary. But we are not dealing with just any approaches: no others can be compared to these two, in terms of their prestige, the duration of their reign, or the influence that they have exercised. These examples are thus more than examples: they are the two most important interpretive strategies in the history of Western civilization.

The Reversal: When, Why

May we say, then, that the development of philological strategy occurred only during the period examined here, between Spinoza and Wolf, roughly between the end of the seventeenth century and the beginning of the nineteenth? There is abundant evidence, as we know, proving the existence of philological techniques from the high classical period onward, and more particularly from the Alexandrian school on. But in the history of ideas one is obliged to distinguish between the first formulation of a thesis and its advent in the properly historical sense. A long road separates the marginal enunciation of an idea and the establishment of a doctrine, the day when an idea is expressed and the day when it is heard; the history of ideas coincides with the history of the reception of ideas, not with that of their production.

So it is with the history of hermeneutics. The rules and techniques that Spinoza codified into a program existed long before his time, in practice and in theory, in Christian exegesis and in the rabbinical gloss. But they never became a battle plan (they could not have done so); the best proof is precisely their coexistence with patristic exegesis. From the moment Spinoza formulated his program, coexistence was no longer possible: one of the two approaches had to disappear, from this particular terrain at least. And that is what happened: philology emerged victorious from the struggle. There is thus indeed a historical phenomenon, which is the replacement of one strategy by another. The two may always have existed and may exist forever; there was nevertheless a conflict whose historical enactment was relatively precise. And if one does not wish, as I do not, to explain the history of ideas exclusively by the relations of ideas among themselves, one must wonder what historical factors made it possible for philology to overturn patristic exegesis precisely in that period.

Among all the events of the era, which ones shall we choose in order to establish a historical correlation with the change observed in the history of hermeneutics? To find an answer, we have to begin by bringing the opposition between patristic exegesis and philology back to its basic terms. The first depends on the possibility of calling upon a truth recognized by all, one that, in order to simplify things, we have labeled Christian doctrine. The second appears as man's reaction to a world in which there is no longer a universal standard. In a hierarchical world, dominated by an absolute truth (and by those who believe in it), it is enough to measure each particular object against a single scale of immutable values, in order for its integration (and thus its interpretation) to be launched. In a democratic society, on the contrary, methodological constraints—and no longer constraints relative to content—must be brought to bear upon the very working of each operation; the relativism of values has to be counterbalanced by methodological codification.

Now it is precisely this reversal that is produced in Europe in the period that interests us. To put it in a single sentence making no claim to historical rigor, the closed world of feudal Christian society gives way to the new bourgeois societies, proclaiming the equality of individuals; no new value comes to play the role, for example, of Christian doctrine in the old system: it is not a question of a redistribution of roles, but of a new scenario. Better still: bringing together two widely separated links in a chain of relations that is nonetheless a single chain, I shall say that it is not by chance that philological doctrine was born in one of the first bourgeois cities of Europe, Amsterdam. The tolerance of the new capitalist society was required for Spinoza to set up as a program what had until then been only underground practices.

Such a line of argument was developed, moreover, by Spinoza himself, to justify his new method, within the *Tractatus Theologico-Politicus.*

> And herein we believe that we see another proof of the excellence of the method we have proposed for arriving at a knowledge of the Scriptures. For assuming as we do that the supreme right to interpret the Bible belongs to every one individually, we conclude that the standard of interpretation should be nothing but the natural light or understanding which is common to all, and not any supernatural light, nor any extrinsic authority. [P. 168]

His method is best because it allows each individual to carry out the work of interpretation without reference to a common and absolute value. The defense of the philological method is equivalent here to a proclamation of the liberty and equality of man. The advent of philology has to occur at this time, and could have occurred at no other.

Typology of Strategies

Patristic exegesis and philology are two types of interpretative strategy. We might wonder also whether they are *the only types* possible, and how they are interrelated: we would thus pass from the historical to the typological perspective.

To interpret always consists in equating two texts (the second of which need not be set forth explicitly): the author's and the interpreter's. The act of interpreting thus necessarily implies two successive choices. The first is whether or not to impose constraints on the association of the two texts. If one chooses to impose constraints, then one must choose whether to attach them to the text one is starting with (the input), to the text one ends up with (the output), or to the trajectory linking the two.

Not to impose any constraints concerning the interpretive act signifies that one is placing oneself at the outer limit of interpretation, in what is sometimes condescendingly called "impressionist criticism." The most characteristic example of this behavior is the free association of the patient on the analyst's couch. Not that rules of association do not exist; they do, but they are not explicit, which is precisely what allows the "unconscious" to surface in this context. Ordinarily, rather than considering it as an interpretation of the input text, we have a tendency to treat the output text itself as the object of interpretation.

Constraints may bear on the *choice of input text* alone without any additional rules bearing upon other points. This attitude underlies the practice of nonverbal symbolism in particular: as for example with those prognosticators who make a narrow choice of the matter to be interpreted, lines on the palm or flights of birds, animal entrails or the configuration of the planets. But we can also see this type of strategy in the interpretation of verbal symbolism, as when we declare that only literary works deserve analysis.

Although both are possible and even frequently encountered, neither of these approaches plays an important role in the history of hermeneutics, doubtless because they still leave such a margin of liberty in interpretation that one cannot speak, in these instances, of strategy in the strict sense; no hermeneutic school is satisfied with so few requirements. The two types of interpretation that abound in the history of hermeneutics, on the other hand, correspond to the two remaining possibilities: imposing constraints on the *operations* that connect the input text with the output text or else on the *output text* itself. Two major types of interpretation: those that I have in fact called operational interpretation (such as philology) and finalist interpretation (such as patristic exegesis). Philology and patristic exegesis are thus not only two examples of interpretive strategies; they represent the two major types of possible strategies.

Each of these types naturally possesses other representatives: to see this, it suffices to change the nature of the operational constraints in the one case, and in the other that of the contents which are the obligatory output.

To take examples closer to us in time than patristic exegesis and philology, we are dealing with finalist interpretations in the case of Marxist or Freudian criticism. In both of these instances the destination is known in advance, and cannot be modified: it consists in principles drawn from the work of Marx or Freud (it is significant that these types of criticism bear the name of their source of inspiration; it is impossible to modify the output text without betraying the doctrine, thus without abandoning it). Whatever work is being analyzed will illustrate the postulates at the end of the road. It goes without saying that this global relationship is coupled with numerous differences which must not be ignored: in the patristic perspective, *certain* texts selected (the sacred ones) proclaim Christian truth; in the Marxist perspective, *all* texts bear witness to Marxist truth.

A modern example of operational interpretation is what is called structural analysis as it has been practiced on myths by Claude Lévi-Strauss or Marcel Détienne, on poetry by Roman Jakobson and Nicolas Ruwet. It is no longer the result that is given in advance, but rather the form of the operations to which one has the right to subject the text being analyzed. These operations deviate hardly at all from the program set forth by Spinoza, moreover: philology and structural analysis simply carry out different parts of this program. We have seen that philology had gradually omitted the category of "intratextual relations"; structural analysis for its part often puts the historical context into parentheses; the difference is, once again, one of *stress* and *emphasis*, not of structure.

Reformulation of the Opposition

One may wonder, however, whether these strategies of interpretation are really what they seem. The question occurred in particular to Spinoza's commentators, who wanted to know whether his demand for an interpretation free of all ideology was realized in his own work, since, alongside the declarations of principle, the pages of the *Tractatus* contain numerous concrete analyses of the Bible. The response is unanimous. Isaac Husik writes: "Spinoza attempts to show that the Bible agrees with his philosophy, as Maimonides tried to show that the Bible agreed with Aristotle's philosophy," and Sylvain Zac: "Spinoza . . . reads Scripture in such a way that one can read the consequences of his own philosophy between the lines. . . . He . . . makes the same error that he criticizes in Maimonides: he explains the texts allegorically and rethinks Christianity in the light of his own philosophy."[1] In spite of his philological professions of faith, Spinoza's interpretation is thus as finalist as that of his adversaries: whatever text is analyzed, it illustrates Spinozian thought. Conversely, however often Augustine may declare that only the destination counts, not the path chosen, it remains no less true that, consciously or not, he and the other founders of patristic exegesis favor or avoid certain types of interpretive operations; so much is clear, even though the explicit codification of these practices falls to others who come afterward.

The opposition between the two interpretive strategies does not disappear for all that, but is moved to another level. No interpretation is free from ideological presuppositions, and no interpretation is arbitrary in its operations. The difference lies, however, in the way the clear and obscure parts of the activity are distributed. Those who practice operational interpretation, be it philology or structural analysis, under the impetus of their own claim to be scientific, forget the presence of an ideology (which, though it may often have little impact, nevertheless does exist) and concentrate their attention on methodological requirements; this accounts for an inevitable proliferation of methodological writings. In turn, the practitioners of finalist interpretation neglect the nature of the operations they are undertaking, and are content to set forth principles that they believe to be illustrated by all the texts analyzed. An uneven distribution, then, of zones of light and shade, or suppression and explicitness, rather than an exclusive presence of one sort of requirement or another. An unevenness of emphasis, merely; it is responsible, nevertheless, for the vicissitudes of the history of hermeneutics.

[1]Isaac Husik, *Philosophical Essays* (Oxford, 1952), "Maimonides and Spinoza on the Interpretation of the Bible," p. 158; Sylvain Zac, *Spinoza et l'interprétation de l'Ecriture* (Paris, 1965), pp. 174, 193.

169

My Strategy?

I should like to raise one last question before bringing my journey to a close. Assuming that we admit the historical determination suggested above, how are we to explain the *coexistence* of the two types of strategy—thus, today, of structural analysis and Marxist analysis? What is determinism worth, if the same causes do not always produce the same effects? And, still more concretely, where am I to situate myself in this dichotomy of method and of content, since it is obvious that, in reading the authors of the past, I have embarked upon an interpretive activity? Or even: what position must one occupy in order to be capable of describing *all* interpretive strategies?

The answer to these questions would have to be sought, attentively and patiently, in the following direction: the interaction between strategies of interpretation and social history passes through an essential mediation which is ideology itself. It was not the commerce of the merchants of Amsterdam that gave birth to philology; the ideology of capitalist expansion was a decisive condition for the hermeneutic renewal. In the same way, the coexistence of ideologies in our world—to put it hastily, in terms of what concerns us, that of an individualist ideology and a collectivist ideology—is the necessary condition of the current copresence of interpretive strategies. And it is my historical destiny, if I dare say so, which obliges me to remain in a double exteriority, as if the "outside" had ceased to imply an "inside." It is not superiority, nor necessarily a curse, but instead rather a characteristic of our time in particular: that of being able to agree with each of the opposing camps, and not to be able to choose between them—as if the distinctive feature of our civilization were the suspension of choice and the tendency to *understand* everything without *doing* anything.

Brief Bibliography

The vastness of the territory and the abundance of the literature devoted to it would make it useless to attempt to put together anything like a complete bibliography on the "symbolics of language." So I shall content myself with pointing out some works which have played an important role in the formation of my own ideas, or else make it possible to orient oneself among the various schools and tendencies which have existed or which still exist. Other pertinent references are provided in two of my previously published studies that can be considered preliminary versions of the present discussion (and thus as now outdated): "Introduction à la symbolique," *Poétique*, 11 (1972), 273–308, and "Le Symbolisme linguistique," in *Savoir, faire, espérer: Les limites de la raison* (Brussels, 1976), pp. 593–622. My book *Les Genres du discours* (Paris, 1978) includes analyses that illustrate many of the notions described here.

Historical Works

Kunjunni Raja, K. *Indian Theories of Meaning*. Madras, 1963. An overview of medieval Sanskrit theories.

Pépin, Jean *Mythe et allégorie*. Paris, 2d ed., 1975. Greek and Christian origins.

Ricoeur, Paul. *The Rule of Metaphor: Multidisciplinary Studies of the Creation of Meaning in Language*, trans. Robert Czerny et al. Toronto and Buffalo, 1977. An overview of contemporary Anglo-Saxon and French theories.

Sørenson, Bengt Algot. *Symbol und Symbolismus in der ästhetischen Theorien des 18. Jahrh. und der deutschen Romantik.* Copenhagen, 1963. A particularly fertile period: German Preromanticism and romanticism.

Szondi, Peter. *Einführung in die literarische Hermeneutik.* Frankfurt, 1975. The history of the passage from religious hermeneutics to literary hermeneutics, in the eighteenth and nineteenth centuries in Germany.

Todorov, Tzvetan. *Theories of the Symbol,* trans. Catherine Porter. Ithaca, 1982. Some particularly important theories: Augustine, classical rhetoric, the German romantics, Freud.

Theoretical Studies

Booth, Wayne. *A Rhetoric of Irony.* Chicago, 1974.

Dubois, Jacques, et al. *Rhétorique générale.* Paris, 1970.

Ducrot, Oswald. *Dire et ne pas dire.* Paris, 1972.

Empson, William. *The Structure of Complex Words.* London, 1951.

Grice, H. P. "Logic and Conversation." In P. Cole and J. L. Morgan, ed., *Syntax and Semantics,* vol. III, *Speech Acts.* New York, 1975. Pp. 41–58.

Henle, Paul. "Metaphor." In P. Henle, ed., *Language, Thought and Culture.* Ann Arbor, 1958. Pp. 173–195.

Hirsch, E. D. *Validity in Interpretation.* New Haven, 1967.

Jurjānī, ʿAbd al-Qāhir al. *Asrār al-balāgha, The Mysteries of Eloquence,* ed. H. Ritter. Istanbul, 1954.

Kerbrat-Orecchioni, Catherine. *La Connotation.* Lyons, 1977.

Piaget, Jean. *Play, Dreams and Imitation in Childhood,* trans. C. Gattegno and F. M. Hodgson. London, 1962.

Schleiermacher, Friedrich. *Hermeneutik.* Heidelberg, 1959.

Sperber, Dan. *Rethinking Symbolism,* trans. Alice L. Morton. Cambridge, Eng., 1975.

Strauss, Leo. *Persecution and the Art of Writing.* Westport, Conn., 1973.

Strawson, P. H. "Phrase et acte de parole," *Langage,* 17 (1970), 19–33.

Todorov, Tzvetan. "Le Sens des sons." *Poétique,* 11 (1972), 446–462.

Wheelwright, Philip. *Metaphor and Reality.* Bloomington, Ind., 1968.

Index

The distinguished critic Tzvetan Todorov here examines together two aspects of discourse that have been treated more or less separately for the thousands of years that scholars and others have reflected upon the nature of language and communication: the production of discourse, which has been traditionally the domain of rhetoric, and the reception and interpretation of discourse, which has always been the object of hermeneutics. Building upon the insights of his earlier works, particularly *Theories of the Symbol,* Todorov analyzes the diverse theories of symbolism and interpretation that have been elaborated over the centuries and considers their contributions to a general theory of verbal symbolism. He discusses figures as diverse as the Sanskrit philosophers and Aristotle, the German Romantics and contemporary semioticians.

Todorov begins by examining general ideas of linguistic symbolism and the interpretive process. He then turns to a detailed consideration of two of the most influential and pervasive interpretive strategies in Western thought: the patristic exegesis of such thinkers as Augustine and Aquinas, and the philological exegesis